D0487964

THE CURRY COMPANION

Sonja Patel

A THINK BOOK

SUPPORTED BY

Tilda

The Birdwatcher's Companion
by Malcolm Tait and Olive Tayler

The Cook's Companion
by Jo Swinnerton

The Countryside Companion
by Malcolm Tait and Olive Tayler

The Fishing Companion
by Lesley Crawford

The Gardener's Companion
by Vicky Bamforth

The Golfer's Companion
by Chris Martin

The History of Britain Companion
by Jo Swinnerton

The Ideas Companion
by Johnny Acton

The Legal Companion
by Vincent Powell

The Literary Companion
by Emma Jones

The London Companion
by Jo Swinnerton

The Moviegoer's Companion
by Rhiannon Guy

The Politics Companion
Edited by Daisy Sampson

The Sailing Companion
by Miles Kendall

The Shakespeare Companion
by Emma Jones and Rhiannon Guy

The Traveller's Companion
by Georgina Newbery and Rhiannon Guy

The Walker's Companion
by Malcolm Tait

The Whisky Companion
by Tom Quinn

The Wildlife Companion
by Malcolm Tait and Olive Tayler

SERIES EDITORS

Malcolm Tait, Emma Jones, Jo Swinnerton
and Rhiannon Guy

To prepare curry is a painstaking,
spiritually elevating process.
Joyeeta Dutta Ray,
Indian journalist and author

THINK
BOOKS

A Think Book

First published in Great Britain in 2006 by
Think Publishing
The Pall Mall Deposit
124-128 Barlby Road, London W10 6BL
www.thinkpublishing.co.uk

Distributed in the UK and Ireland by Macmillan Distribution Ltd.,
Brunel Road, Houndsmills, Basingstoke RG21 6XS

Distributed in the United States and Canada by
Sterling Publishing Co., Inc.
387 Park Avenue South
New York, NY 10016-8810

Text © Think Publishing 2006
Design and layout © Think Publishing 2006
The moral rights of the author have been asserted

Author: Sonja Patel
Companion team: Tania Adams, Victoria Chow,
James Collins, Rica Dearman, Louise Fanthorpe, Emma Jones,
Lou Millward, Matt Packer and Fay Warrilow.

ISBN-10: 1-84525-034-6
ISBN-13: 978-1-84525-034-8

Printed in Italy by Grafica Veneta S.p.A.

The spice must flow.
Frank Herbert, US author

THANKS

Anybody who has ever written or raved about curry, in particular the ramblings, research and recipes of Pat Chapman, Madhur Jaffrey, Lizzie Collingham, David Burton, Mrs Beeton and Dean Mahomet.

Miria Swain and Tom Harris for their hot haute cuisine and extensive library of cookbooks; the British Library for theirs.

Maureen and Dinker Patel, for a lifetime of biryani.

Jean-Philippe Tremblay, a rare and precious spice.

Sincere thanks go out to the Think Interns who added their own touches of spice to this book: Daniele Bora, Tristan Cox, David Kircaldy, Rachel Lin and Alex O'Hagan.

Bandy the word 'curry' about – as I did to almost anyone who would listen when the first ingredients for *The Curry Companion* were thrown into the pot – and watch modern meltdown turn to welcome relief as they finally remember what they didn't know they wanted to eat tonight (mine's a chicken korma and a peshwari naan from Joy Authentic Indian Cuisine in Broadway Market, just for the record).

For some, curry is more than just a comforting takeaway or ready-meal from M&S, however. It's more than just another hot dish. It's a vast melting pot of political, geographical, metaphysical and anthropological intrigue that has scoured the world for its wealth of ingredients, crossed oceans in search of the perfect flavours and spun its spicy tale through the centuries. Touted as both the 'nation's favourite dish' and nothing more than a 'colonial casserole', it provokes controversy, but also crosses social boundaries and metaphysical borders. In short, this saucy number is one hot topic – some might even say addictive – that provides more than a little food for thought.

What, might you ask, is curry and where did it come from? Who 'invented' chicken tikka masala? What's the hottest curry you can eat? Who are the King and Queen of Curry? What is the difference between a Thai curry and a Malaysian? Why is there a curry museum in Japan? Can curry help cure cancer? Why are there so many baltis in Birmingham? What is the best way to cook rice? Is curry a national treasure or will it be the death of a nation? Are Edwina Curry and Tim Curry related? And more to the point, why curry and chips and what are those coloured bits in a pilau?

In answer to some of these questions, historic texts and ancient cookery books were dragged out and dusted down from the archives. Chefs were brought in to discuss the merits of curry powder and create one-off recipes. Brick Lane and the streets of Southall became more than familiar haunts. Waistlines expanded. And family members were even blackmailed into divulging the secrets of their prize biryani. In the quest for the ultimate curry companion, the aim was to leave no tandoor oven, flock-papered palace or pestle and mortar unturned.

The end result is a delicious masala of fact (most of it), fable (the tasty bit) and fiction (well maybe just a spicy extract or two) with which it's hoped to tempt even the most insatiable curry hunger. Whether you use *The Curry Companion* to enthral fellow diners, brush up on your paratha pronunciation or engage it as a post-curry digestive is up to you...

Sonja Patel, Author

THE WIT AND WISDOM OF TIM CURRY

You might expect a little bit more from an Emmy award-winning British actor...

But we live in a modern world, you know, and, and also it does seem to me that if you – that whatever talents you have, it... I mean it may sound a bit absurd but I, I think it's your, absolutely your duty to resolve them, you know?

One of the best things that ever happened to me was Rocky Horror being a total flop in New York as a play. I mean, it was a disaster, and it was the night of the long knives as far as the critics were concerned.

The people on the business side in the music business are kind of different from the theatre business. I think it's partly because there are different pressures on the industries.

Um, musicians are funnier you know, than actors on the whole. You see, there are always purists in every, in every art form and particularly, I think, in in performance arts of any kind.

CRAZY IN LOVE – WITH CURRY

Oh, Beyoncé, you came, you saw, you conquered, and you fell in love – with curry. We can forgive you that. It's tasty, some say it's addictive, and it can be undeniably hot. But fly it all the way from Surrey to New York? Surely you could have got someone to cook you a nice tikka masala for half the price (£4,000 say celebrity gossips). You can blame it on your Virgin Record chief – the papers did, although we're going on reports from the *Daily Star* here, albeit via the *Indian Times* (for whom the story was too exciting to bear). Allegedly, said chief tracked down the takeaway, Lingfield Tandoori – tried and tested by the Spice Girls. They of all people should know their stuff, with a name like that. It was sad to hear your personal trainer has now reportedly banned you from the stuff to help you get your flatter-than-flat stomach back. Hopefully, he will find a recipe for a tasty low-cal vegetable and lentil curry that you can cook up at home yourself. You don't have to cut curry out. Maybe give kormas and dhansaks a wide birth for now. Find a new curry companion: Slimming World do a curry book. True curry love will find a way. Good luck and curry back.

---

10 *Amount of time in minutes it takes pure basmati to cook compared to an average of 20 minutes for potatoes*

Coriander

A relative of parsley and therefore cumin, coriander – another major component of many curry dishes, curry powders and garam masalas, and thought to be one of the world's most ancient used spices – hails from Morocco, Romania and Greece and found its way across Europe and the Middle East to Asia and into curries via ancient spice-trading routes. Sanskrit writings talk of coriander as early as 1,500BC, although the spice could hail back as far as 5,000BC with ancient Greek writings citing it as both food and digestive remedy. The Bible's Old Testament (Exodus 16:31) also mentions the spice with a reference to manna '...being white like coriander seed'. What most people don't known is that coriander refers only to the seed of the plant *Corinadrum sativum* – the leafy part should actually be referred to as cilantro. Although both spice and herb come from the same plant the flavours are not interchangeable, with delicate palates especially noting a distinct difference between the two. Both components are used in popular curries, however, with the lemon-sage aromatic of coriander combining perfectly with other hot and fragrant spices. The fresh, sometimes musky cilantro leaves are used as a garnish or in salads and can really help to cool things down when that vindaloo or madras finally becomes too hot to handle.

GLOBAL WARMING: INDONESIA

On the spice trail and around the world on the good ship Curry...

From Sumatra to Bali, 'curry' developed with the help of Indian (Java was even mentioned in India's ancient *Ramayana* as *yava-dvipa*) and Arab traders (Indonesia now incorporates the clove-rich Spice Islands of Maluku) and then European rule (namely the Dutch in Sumatra and Java). Island life across the archipelago and in coastal regions dictates a wide range of curried seafood including crab, shrimp and fish; likewise, curried wild boar is *de rigeur* in the Kalimantan jungle. One of the most well-known Indonesian dishes is rendang, a spicy beef (or buffalo, as Lonely Planet's *World Food Indonesia* (2002) enthuses about it) stew or 'curry' that uses galangal – a native ginger-like rhizome used widely in south-east Asia – Indonesian bay leaves, chilli, garlic, ginger and, of course, coconut milk. Indonesia also has a classic curry paste with dried coconut, anchovy, caraway, peanut oil and macadamia nuts, while satay – stemming from the Mughal-style kebab – is eaten and used for spiritual purposes on islands such as Bali.

Luigi the abstract painter had hit upon a perfect visual equivalent for his last curry.

MAKE ME A MULLIGATAWNY

Despite its similarity in sound to the Wings hit 'Mull of Kintyre', this spicy soup-cum-curry dish has no direct links with Scotland. In fact, it is said to derive from the Indian Tamil dish *molo tunny*, from the Tamil words *molegoo* meaning 'pepper' and *tunes* meaning 'water'. While the British like to start their meal with soup, *molo tunny* was a watery main dish, not unlike a Japanese *ramen*, spiced with black pepper, chillis and often tamarind for a sour kick. Under colonial influence, minced meat and vegetables were added and the broth morphed into a make-do-and-mend very British dish. Cooked rice, lime wedges, grated coconut, fried bacon and hard-boiled eggs were often to be found as pick-and-choose garnishes. Mulligatawny's fame spread from Madras to other parts the Empire, and soon the soup de la jour was served at every banquet, party and ball. Back in Britain, where 'real soup' was a fixture on menus, it was often deemed too hot or too watery for distinguished palates. Today, chefs like Jamie Oliver are morphing it further into modern cuisine with recipes such as pumpkin rice laksa soup from his bestselling book of 2004, *Jamie's Dinners*.

Baati – round, unleavened bread cooked in desert areas of northern India, often stuffed with onion, peas, ghee and chilli

Bhakri – hard, unleavened bread from western and central India, often made with rice flour and eaten for breakfast

Bahatoora – soft, white bread, generally eaten as an accompaniment to choley, chickpea curry

Chapatti – from south Asia, fried and then brushed with ghee. Often eaten with cooked dahl or vegetable curry

Dosa – southern Indian pancake-type snack, eaten for breakfast

Idli – steamed patties made from black lentils and eaten with chutney

Khakhra – flavoursome bread from north-west India, roasted for added crunchiness

Malabari paratha – layered breads, from Kerala, grilled as dumplings; served with spicy curries

Naan – unleavened bread from north-west India, cooked in a traditional tandoor oven and popular as an accompaniment to balti dishes. Often stuffed with nuts and raisins (peshwari naan), minced meats (keema naan) or potatoes (aloo naan)

Poppadum – wafer-like flatbread, made from lentil, chickpea or rice flour, and traditionally served in curry houses as an appetiser with chutney and mint dips

Paratha – thick flatbread, generally stuffed with vegetables (gobi paratha) and paneer, Indian cheese (paneer paratha)

Puri – unleavened bread from southern Asia, eaten to accompany bean and rice dishes, particularly at special occasions, such as weddings

Roti – the Malaysian word for 'bread' and the term most often used to refer to all kinds of round, flat, Indian breads

Uttapam – the Indian 'pizza', a crispy flat bread, generally covered with tomatoes, chilli and mixed vegetables

---

KNIFE OR SPOON?

Chopsticks may have been introduced to Thailand centuries ago, but most Thais use Western cutlery – although not as we know it. Dining in the country generally involves using a fork and a large spoon, which is held in the right hand instead of a knife.

Age at which Gandhi, India's most famous spiritual leader, got married 13

CURRIED THINKING

I am the black on the outside, clad in a wrinkled cover
And yet within I bear a burning marrow.
I season delicacies, the banquets of kings, and the luxuries of the table,
Both the sauces and the tenderised meats of the kitchen.
But you will find in me no quality of any worth,
Unless your bowels have been rattled by my gleaming marrow.

St Aldham (c. 639-709)

Answer: Pepper

BURNING QUESTIONS

What do the following mean in Thai cuisine?
a) Luak
b) Gaeng
c) Tot
Answer on page 151.

KINKY KEDGEREE
(OR TOM AND MIRIA'S BREAKFAST IN BED)

A recipe designed to curry favour(s) with your loved one. Serves two (or three).

$\frac{1}{2}$ Spanish onion, chopped
Butter
1 cup rice
1 cup cold water
$\frac{1}{2}$ pint milk
1 whole smoked haddock
1 heaped teaspoon Bolst's of Bangalore curry powder (mild)
Flat leaf parsley
Watercress
Lemon
2 eggs
Salt and pepper

1) Fry chopped onion in butter until soft. Add rice and water. Simmer for one minute. Cover and leave on lowest heat.

2) Bring milk to boil. Reduce heat and poach haddock. Flake fish into rice. Stir through curry powder, chopped parsley, watercress, squeeze of lemon and pinch of salt.

3) Serve in bed with poached egg and black pepper on top.

14 *Year in the seventeenth century of the first recorded Bengali settlement in London*

Deciphering the curry house menu...

Tandoor's offspring, 'tikka' actually means 'little thing' and refers to the small, bite-sized pieces of meat that would have originally have come on a kebab skewer. While tikka has been cooking on sub-continental coals for thousands of years, the tikka masala is actually something of a modern invention – originating in the UK. Not content with the brown appearance of tandoored meat, British chefs in the 1970s first added the tartarzine red and yellow food colouring that now flies the flag for not-so-authentic tandoori and tikka masala. Urban myth denotes that the chicken tikka masala or CTM hit the UK scene in the 1980s, when a certain curry house chef (identity unknown) was thought to have added a tomato, cream and spice 'masala' sauce to liven things up. The unsuspecting fellow inadvertently produced a dish that was a hit not just with his own customers, its garish tones and fast-food appeal drew in the eager palates of a glamorous New Romantic nation. Hailed by UK minister Robin Cook as a 'truly British national dish' in a pre-election speed in 2001, the CTM is now a firm favourite on our menus, in our homes, in our sandwiches and even on our crisps and pizzas. Spice manufacturer Patak's even exports its tikka masala paste back to India, a coals-to-Newcastle story of a dish that has gone full circle.

Heat factor: Mild and mellow.

HELP THE CURRY GO DOWN

British Indian restaurants would have you believe that a mint imperial or two is the traditional digestive to eat after a curry. In fact paan – usually a mixture of areca nut (the seed of the areca palm), lime paste (from kiln-baked seashells) and various spices wrapped up in a betel leaf (from a tree-climbing vine) – is the authentic last order of the day. Take a rickshaw ride through the streets of most Asian countries, especially India, and you might be concerned to see your driver's mouth dripping with blood. Worry not, as this is simply the betel juice dripping down. The paan he is eating may well be a way to stave off hunger, as the concoction not only freshens the palate, but increases saliva to help keep pangs at bay. The required spitting that results from sucking on betel (the mixture is not actually chewed, but placed in the cheek gum and sucked for some time) may not be the most civilised act, but swallowing is worse as it can render the opposite effect of heartburn. Street cleaners across the world may see things differently – if a renounced curry doesn't get them, then the betel juice will.

In France, no one's conditioned by Escoffier any more, so why are
we so concerned that this is how a dish was made 200 years ago by
some old git who's been passing the recipe down through one
Lucknowi family? You hear this story everywhere: 'My chef's got
the only recipe because his grandad gave it to him, and his grandad
gave it to him, and his father cooked for the king of so-and-so.'
People say to me, 'Is your food authentic?' And my response is, 'Do
you mean good?' What does authenticity mean anyway? Flies in
your food, cholera, dysentery? It could mean any of those.
Iqbal Wahab, founder of The Cinnamon Club and former
editor of *Tandoori*, quoted in *The Observer Food Monthly*,
12 May 2002

SPICE GUYS

On English attempts to force the Dutch from the
Spice Islands of the Indian Ocean

At Bantam the English and Hollanders had great disputes, insomuch as it was verily thought they would have fought together in the road, for the general of the Hollanders had brought thither fourteen great ships, ready to fight, where the English had nine, which they fitted for defense; but they fought not, for the governor of Bantam forbade them to fight in his road, and threatened them that if they did fight contrary to his command he would cut the throats of all their men that he should find upon the land.

The 27th of November the Hollanders proclaimed war against all the English at the Moluccas, Banda, and Amboyna, threatening to make one and all prize and to put them to the edge of the sword; which proclamation of theirs they fixed upon the doors of their lodgings at Bantam, challenging all to be theirs as their proper inheritance.

As a result of English disappointments with dislodging the Dutch from the Spice Islands, they turned instead to India. In 1614 Sir Thomas Roe was instructed by James I to visit the court of Jahangir, the Mongol emperor of Hindustan. Sir Thomas was to arrange a commercial treaty and to secure for the East India Company sites for commercial agencies, --- 'factories' as they were called. Sir Thomas was successful, and though the Great Moghul Jahangir was contemptuous of the presents sent him by James I, sent [a] remarkably polite letter nonetheless...
Anonymous (a French seaman of the early 1600s), *England, India and The East Indies*, c. 1617

16 *Year in the seventeenth century in which an East Indian was baptised as*
   'Peter' in St Dionis Church, London, as chosen by James I

Edwina Curry, Tim Curry, Adam Curry – it seems bearers of this spicy name are everywhere, although they have nothing to do with the dish. According to www.curry-family.net (a US site, devised by one Will Sherman, apparently also a Curry?) the Gaelic-Irish name is rightfully O'Curry – in fact in native terms it should be O Comhraidhe. Over time, Corry and Corra were thrown into the equation. There are Corrys in Kerricurrehy, County Cork and the name is found in County Kerry, too. Over in County Westmeath, the O Comhraidhes lent their name to Curristown, now Belmont. However, over in Ulster, many a Curry is said to come from Scotland, although in truth they should have stuck to Currie; while County Antrim has a Curry or two in the nineteenth-century barony of Carey. From Corry came O Corraidh or O Corra and from this came Corr (as in those grating Irish warblers, The Corrs). The site goes on to discuss even more stems of the surname Curry, but this can conjure little interest unless you are indeed a Curry – and in this case you should pay the link a visit yourself (or at least check your roots up in the British Library's Family Records Centre). If you're a Curry living over in the States with Will, you're among good company – thanks to extensive Irish immigration there, Curry is the 313th most common name there.

CURRY ROCKS

The past decade has seen a huge migration of skilled hi-tech workers from India to the US on the H-1B visa programme. For many, that old American Dream has lost none of its sparkle, but adapting to life in a foreign country can be harder than expected. One such group of Indian migrants has found a way to share their experiences and add some humour to the visa queue – by putting it all to music. The result – a new East-meets-West groove in English, Hindi and Tamil, that the musicians who made it dub Curry Rock. The multilingual album, released in 2005 is aptly named *H1Bees* with the title track following an Indian worker through the entire process of acquiring a visa, travelling to America and settling down there. Although the lyrics are light-hearted, the subjects they reference are something of a controversy; some American tech workers are claiming the H-1B-holders are stealing their jobs. Although none of the musicians intend to give in to pressure or give up their day jobs, the project's next goals are to try and figure out a way to make their Curry Rock back home in India. A case of like meets like as migrant dish and migrant worker travel full circle.

FLOCK-PAPER FAVOURITES: TANDOORI

Deciphering the curry house menu…

Contrary to popular belief, the 'tandoor' of 'tandoori' actually refers to the oven, not the often technicolour sauce. This cylindrical clay oven, fuelled by charcoal at its base and with a vent at the top, creates the required high temperatures (up to 480°C) to char-cook that curry house favourite, tandoori chicken, to succulent perfection. While the tandoor is unique to the subcontinent, its origins are thought to stem from Egypt where a similar device – the tonir – was used to bake bread. In Persia it became the tanoor and some 2,000 years ago helped to create the first nane lavesh bread and tikkeh kebabs. Mughal rule at the palace of Lahore from the late fifteenth century helped to concoct the addictive marinade of spices, herbs and yoghurt that we know today, with cayenne, chilli or turmeric (depending on the recipe) rendering the original signature red-brown colour. Despite its fragrant flavour, however, tandoori only became popular in central India after partition swept it south from Pakistan in 1947. In the UK it was hyped as a healthy and exotic 1970s snack and tandoori mania was born. In takeaway terms, the spices, marinade and ovens are still there, but the colour/addiction factor is sadly more likely to start with an E.

Heat factor: Mild and mellow.

LEAF IT OUT

Contrary to popular belief (or even be-leaf), neither curry nor curry leaf came first and curry powder is not simply a ground-down form of the plant, nor is curry the dish named after it. (Thou shalt not get a chicken curry by simply adding curry leaf to it.) Native to India, Sri Lanka, Bangladesh and the Andaman Islands, curry leaves are still cultivated there and in other places where migrant Indians went. While British curry powder does not dictate that it be present, the curry leaf is used extensively in southern Indian and Sri Lankan cooking – not just in 'curries', but other meat, veg and fish dishes plus soups, pickles, chutneys and egg variations. In these regions, the ground-down leaf can often appear in powder mixes where fresh leaves are not available or to speed things along. Where the popular concept of 'curry' and the curry leaf meet is in the Tamil word *kari*. An alternative word for the curry leaf in India is *kari-pattha* and it has been mentioned in ancient Tamil literature as far back as 1AD. Simmering on the other hob is curry, believed by many to derive from the same word. Whether or not you decide to put curry leaf in your curry is up to you.

BURNING QUESTIONS

What are the main ingredients of 'mutter paneer'?
Answer on page 151.

QUOTE UNQUOTE

Me and me mum and me dad and me gran
We're off to Waterloo
Me and me mum and me dad and me gran
And a bucket of vindaloo
Keith Allen, British comedian and author, from his profound
1998 alternative England World Cup anthem, 'Vindaloo'

THE CULINARY ADVENTURES OF
DEAN MAHOMET

Letter XXVII: *On the practice of chewing betel, recorded while in Bombay circa 1778...*

'As the practice of chewing betel is universal throughout India, the description of it may not prove unentertaining. It is a creeping plant cultivated in the same manner as the vine, with leaves full of large fibres like those of the citron, but longer and narrower at the extremity. It is mixed with the arek and chunam before it is used. The arek-nut is exactly in form and bigness like a nutmeg, only harder: it is marbled in the inside with white and reddish streaks, and wrapped up in the leaf. Chunam is nothing more than burnt lime made of the finest shells. To these three articles is often added for luxury, what they call cachoonda, a japan earth,

which from perfumes and other mixtures, receives a high improvement. The taste of it is, at first, little better than that of common chalk, but soon turns to a flavor that dwells agreeably on the palate...

So prevalent is the custom of chewing betel, that it is used by persons of every description; but it is better prepared for people of condition, who consider it a breach of politeness to take leave of their friends, without making presents of it. No one attempts to address his superior, unless his mouth is perfumed with it; and to neglect this ceremony even with an equal, would be deemed an unpardonable rudeness.

'The dancing girls are eternally scented with it, as being a powerful incentive to love...'
Dean Mahomet, *The Travels of Dean Mahomet,* **1794**

A nineteenth-century guide to spices and their main uses in Anglo-Indian food

Spice	Nice for...
Allspice (pimento or Jamaican pepper)	Worcester sauce
Aromatic spice (pepper, salt, cinnamon, mace, bay leaf, thyme, marjoram, nutmeg, cayenne)	Braised meat and game pies
Bay leaves	Stocks, custards, blanc-manges
Cayenne pepper	Heating curry and soup
Celery	Used fresh or to flavour soup
Cinnamon	Sweet drinks and sweet dishes
Cloves	Soups, sauces and puddings
Coriander	Curry powder/fresh leaves for soups, salads
Curry powder	Spices for soups, stews, sauces; 'It is hot'
Lemons and limes	All dishes
Mace (husk of nutmeg)	Soups, stews, sauces
Mint	Pea soup, mint sauce or potatoes
Mustard	Energy, appetite and as a condiment
Nutmeg	Sweet and savoury, sparingly used
Parsley	Sauces, stews, stuffings and as a garnish
Pepper (common)	Use in all meat dishes
Sage	Oily meats such as pork or goose
Salt	All used, highly important in the field
Sugar (coarse brown in India)	Very nutritious, preserves fruit, sweetens food
Thyme	Stews and soups
Turmeric	Curry powder, gives bright yellow colour
Vanilla	Cakes and custards
Mixed herbs (basil, marjoram, parsley, savoury and thyme)	Rissoles, mince rolls, beef olives
Mixed spice	Cinnamon, cloves, ginger, mace and nutmeg sausages, bread pudding, Christmas pudding

20 *Year in the twentieth century when the first Indian restaurant in East London was established*

GLOBAL WARMING:
LAOS, CAMBODIA AND VIETNAM

On the spice trail and around the world on the good ship Curry...

The three principal countries of former French Indochina saw a succession of Indian-influenced kingdoms for the first 1,300 years AD. Hindu Brahmins, Buddhists monks, scholars and craftsmen fused their religion, language, artistry and cuisine with local culture creating a melting pot of tastes and styles. A visit to Angkor Wat in Cambodia, for example, reveals the vast impression of Hindu and Buddhist cultures on its walls. With the French – who captured and ruled various parts of the region between 1884-1954, came an Indian workforce, drafted from French-Indian colonies such as Pondicherry and Mahe. Vietnamese curries often have a distinct southern Indian flavour, often flavoured with curry leaves. A French-style stew of carrots and potatoes might be curried with spicy curry powder or paste. Others swayed under the nearby influences of China are more like a Chinese stir-fry, but with the addition of curry powder, fish sauce (here called *nuoc mam*) and lemon grass. Rice also gets the spice treatment with cloves, star anise, onion, ginger, coconut milk, cashews and raisins, although noodles and French bread – a surprise to many Westerners – are also popular ways to mop the curry up.

AYE, AYE, COUNTRY CAPTAIN

Search for 'country captain' on the web and you'll be sent to deepest southern America, where the dish is often mistakenly believed to have originated from (add 'uk' and you get the Middlesex Cricket Club and more than a few references to Captain Cook). As David Burton explains in his book *The Raj at Table* (1993), this 'most celebrated chicken dish' is, in fact, another Anglo-Indian dish: 'The term "country" used to refer to anything Indian… and hence the country captain after whom this dish is named may have been in charge of sepoys.' He goes on to say that the captain was probably more likely to have been in charge of a country boat, 'since the recipe turned up midway through the nineteenth century at ports as far apart as Liverpool and the American South'. Now the route is becoming clearer. A known favourite of another country captain, US President Franklin Roosevelt when served up by a cook in Georgia, another American fan salivates over serving it with his Grandma Clarke's currant tarts. An interesting suggestion to go with a meal made with roast chicken, ghee, ginger, onions, garlic, turmeric, black pepper, chillis, lemons and stock water… team at your will.

The 'Lahore'
In the words of that literary Raj, Rudyard Kipling,
some things are 'just so'…

Legend goes that Lahore was named in the sake of Loh (*Luv* in Sanskrit), son of Rama, hero of the Hindu epic Ramayana. It is one of Pakistan's major cities and the capital of the province of Punjab. The first Mughal Emperor, Akbar, built the famous Lahore Fort in the Persian style with the monumental Badshahi Masjid and Alamgiri Gate added by the last Emperor, Aurangzeb.

In the eighteenth and nineteenth centuries, the city was ruled by the Sikhs and became the capital of sovereign Punjab, before coming under British rule. It finally fell to Pakistan after the partition of 1947. Like the architecture, the local cuisine is a masala of Middle Eastern, pre-Mughal and colonial influences with grilled or barbecued meats taking centre stage on the menu – chiefly kebabs, localised with strong Indian spices, lemon juice and yoghurt.

Of course, for cricket fans, Lahore is the birthplace of Pakistani legend Imran Khan. For many, a classic chicken curry with tomatoes and onions, down the local Lahore is a fine way to wrap up a match – as long as the Pakistanis don't win, that is.

It also seems there's a Lahore for every occasion, with Lahore Kebab House in London's Whitechapel, Lahore Dreams over in Tooting and the Lahore Palace in Darmstadt, Germany.

A precursor to Emperor Shajahan's Taj Mahal, the Lahore Palace was built in the grounds of the fort as a rather large token of love for his wife Mumtaz Mahal. Inlayed with thousands of intricately cut and multi-coloured mirrors it stands as reflective proof that, just like a good Lahori curry, all that glitters is not gold.

QUOTE UNQUOTE

Many people consider [the Harappa Culture] the world's first gourmets and creative cooks. Their achievements may be measured by the fact that their seasonings were adopted by all who came after them.
William Laas, US author of *Cuisines of the Western World* on the ancient Indus Valley (now Pakistan), spice masters who were making curries 6,000 years ago

*The lack of hot spices in a korma can often
cause bouts of depression.*

SPICE GUYS

Pinpointing the lure of exploration

Men have travelled, as they have lived, for religion, for wealth, for
knowledge, for pleasure, for power and the overthrow of rivals. Yet
no very profound acquaintance with Hakluyt's book [an explorer's
journal compiled by the famed collector of overseas travel narratives,
Richard Hakluyt] is needed to discern, as he clearly discerned, the
single thread of interest running through all these pilgrimages. The
discovery of the new Western World followed, as an incidental
consequence, from the long struggle of the nations of Europe for
commercial supremacy and control of the traffic with the East. In all
these dreams of the politicians and merchants, sailors and
geographers, who pushed back the limits of the unknown world,
there is the same glitter of gold and precious stones, the same odour
of far-fetched spices. (1605)

Sir Walter Raleigh, from his personal journals

*The Bangladeshis created the Indian restaurant market in the UK.
Without the Bangladeshis the wave of smart Indian restaurants we
are experiencing now wouldn't be here.*
Amin Ali, owner of the Red Fort curry house in Soho, London,
quoted in the *The Observer Food Monthly*,
8 December 2002

HOW THE CURRY HOUSE GOT ITS NAME

The 'Ganges'
*In the words of that literary Raj, Rudyard Kipling,
some things are 'just so'…*

When India's first prime minister Jawaharlal Nehru spoke of his country's sacred river as: 'a symbol of India's age-long culture and civilisation, ever changing, ever flowing and yet ever the same', he could almost have been talking about curry – one stemming from the Gangotri Glacier in the Uttaranchal Himalayas and the other from a melting pot of culture blended over thousands of years of civilisation and rule. The river flows a total length of 2,510 kilometres and forms a large and fertile basin stretching across north India and what is now Bangladesh, before pouring out into the Bay of Bengal. Often referred to as Ma Ganga or Mother Ganges – legend goes that the goddess poured herself down from heaven upon the ashes of King Sagara's sons (Sagara being the first 'ruler of earth') before raising them up again. She now supports one of the highest densities of human population in the world and in turn, is said to wash away the sins of those who bathe within her waters. The most sacred banks are at Benares or Varanasi, also a popular cremation spot (for those who can't afford charcoal, corpses are thrown in semi-grilled). As testament to her pious pull, in 2001 over 70 million Hindus came together during the Kumbh Mela, to worship Ma Ganga's waters in the holy city of Allahabad. It is also believed that drinking water from the Ganges at a human's last breath will take the soul to heaven. The first Mughal Emperors wouldn't drink anything else, with Emperor Akbar declaring it 'the water of immortality' – he would find a way to transport the precious liquid even if he was 300 kilometres away in the Punjab. Some puritan fans of their local Ganges – whether it be in Swindon, East Sussex, Montreal, Bangor or Paraty, Brazil – may well do the same, travelling hours back home to feed their weary souls with a heaven-sent korma.

It is not uncommon to make a not-so-fowl error over the Bombay duck. Despite its feathery name, it is in fact a fish, and an Indian delicacy at that. The source of this fish does prove its name half right, with the salty side dish originating from the costal city of Bombay (now Mumbai). No one seems to know exactly how this curry companion got its name, but it is thought to refer to the way the finned one swims so near the surface of the water, like a duck. What can be derived from scrawlings of the late nineteenth century is that is was known as a dish by then. As described in David Burton's *The Raj at Table*: 'The name is certainly very old, for the seventeenth century British residents of Bombay were nicknamed "ducks".' To this day, the tit-bit fish – also called bummalos or bombloes – are hung out and dried by their heads on the beaches of fishing villages in Mumbai. Although banned from Britain's menus by the European Commission (EC) after the salmonella scare (nothing to do with the fish salmon) in 1996, 'duck'-addicted businessman, David Delaney from Hereford, fought to bring them back. He succeeded in 2000, with the EC agreeing to their import, as long as they were packed in an 'EC approved' packing station after drying on the beach. You are now free to crumble the Bombay duck into or onto your curry and rice – at your peril.

MRS BEETON'S CURRY WISDOM

Curried Mutton

Ingredients: The remains of any joint of cold mutton, 2 onions, $\frac{1}{4}$lb of butter, 1 dessertspoonful of curry powder, 1 dessertspoonful of flour, salt to taste, $\frac{1}{4}$ pint of stock or water.

Mode: Slice the onions in thin rings, and put them into a stewpan with the butter, and fry of a light brown; stir in the curry powder, flour, and salt, and mix all well together. Cut the meat into nice thin slices (if there is not sufficient to do this, it may be minced), and add it to the other ingredients; when well browned, add the stock or gravy, and stew gently for about $\frac{1}{2}$ hour. Serve in a dish with a border of boiled rice, the same as for other curries.

Time – $\frac{1}{2}$ hour.

Average cost – exclusive of the meat, 6d.

Seasonable – in winter.

Isabella Beeton – aka 'Mrs Beeton',
Book of Household Management, 1861

Cumin

The pale green seed of the *cuminum cyminum* – or cumin – is never far away from a curry – or at least finds its way into side-dish seasoning or rice. Small and elliptical, cumin is actually part of the parsley family and native to the shores of Egypt and the Mediterranean Sea (although it is now grown in many hot places in the world including India, China, northern Africa and the Americas). A spice with biblical reverence, it is mentioned in the Bible's Old Testament; cumin has also been found as a food-stuff and pampering ingredient in ancient Roman texts and was a favourite way to spice things up in conquested countries and in the Middle East – it is prevalent in Morocco. One story goes that cumin was also associated with greed and that is how the Roman Emperor Marcus Aurelius got the nickname Cuminus. While cumin may seem like a new spice that found its way to the UK via the curry concoctions of the British Raj, it has in fact been present in our cuisine since medieval times. Similarly in Mexico, cumin has been a staple ingredient of chilli con carne and tamales for centuries. The warm yet bitter flavour can be obtained from the seeds, when fried in butter or oil; or enhanced further by grinding the seeds into a fine powder – a component of both curry powder and the curry constituent garam masala.

GLOBAL WARMING: EAST AFRICA

On the spice trail and around the world on the good ship Curry...

Trading across the Indian Ocean has always been rife, providing exchanges of spices and the cross-pollination of dishes. Following the British colonisation of India and other Asian countries, the European scramble to own parts of Africa culminated in British East Africa, which ruled over several regions including Kenya, Uganda, Tanganyika and Zanzibar (the latter two joined in 1964 to become Tanzania). The Indian workforce was recruited once again and together with the British colonial taste for 'curry' established a number of Asian-influenced dishes, alongside earlier Persian inspirations such as pilaf (the first settlers in East Africa were Arabs). In particular, many Gujaratis travelled from India to Kenya and Uganda, many to work on the railroads there. Rags-to-riches stories of those who started selling dahls and ended up with vast amounts of property are not uncommon. Their adoption of the Swahili language resulted in native dishes such as kuku paka – chicken and coconut. The much-loved mogo or cassava is also a favourite, fried or used in curries along with okra and lamb.

In October 2002, India's infamous 'Curry Western', Ramesh Sippy's *Sholay*, was dubbed top of the Bollywood pile by the British Film Institute. Roughly translated as 'Embers, Flames, Flames of the Sun', the hit film – still India's highest grossing film of all time – drew on a number of influences including Sergio Leone's spaghetti western *The Magnificent Seven*, itself inspired by Akira Kurosawa's *The Seven Samurai*. The recipe of the film involves a retired police office Thakur (Sanjeev Kumar) who hires two convicts Veeru and Jai (Dharmendra and Amitabh Bachchan) – based on Butch Cassidy and the Sundance Kid – to capture Gabbar Singh, who is responsible for killing Thakur's entire family, except himself and his daughter-in-law. Outlaw violence is as rife as a hot vindaloo and spice is added by a two-pronged love affair, including Veeru's love for the grief-stricken widow Radha. Of course, even a Curry Western wouldn't be complete without some Bollywood-style comedy and song and dance sequences. The vitriolic chase comes to a heated climax when Thakur kills Gabbar with his spike-heeled shoes. Well, that's the director's cut anyway – shocked censors at the time made him change it to show the policeman leading him away to jail.

CURRIED WORDS

Curry houses are not the first things which spring to mind when Leamington Spa is mentioned. But it was, in fact, one of the first provincial English towns to have a selection of Indian restaurants. A visitor in 1975 enthused, 'There are restaurants and delicatessens in a dozen national styles. Yams and tortillas, cabanos and cracowska, grappa and pitta bread can be found with ease... [this] is not the normal state of affairs in medium-sized English provincial towns; and to someone like me, who comes from a town where they have only just heard about green peppers, it makes Leamington seem like London and New York rolled into one compact sample-sized city... the existence of five Indian restaurants – as well as upwards of 50 other eating places – seems to suggest a level of luxury and extravagance to tempt the fate of Sodom and Gomorrah.' Leamington's proximity to Coventry and Birmingham, where many of Britain's Bangladeshi and Pakistani immigrants found work in the car industry, made it, where Indian food was concerned, one of Britain's pioneering towns. It still is.

Lizzie Collingham,
Curry: A Tale of Cooks and Conquerors, 2006

KNOW YOUR INDIAN MENU: VEGETABLES

Aloo .... Potato

Bhindi .... Okra

Brinjel .... Aubergine

Chana .... Chick peas

Dahl .... Lentils

Gobi .... Cauliflower

Lobia .... Black-eyed beans

Maash .... Lentils

Matter .... Peas

Palak .... Spinach

Paneer .... Asian cheese

Rajma .... Red kidney beans

Sag .... Spinach

CURRIED WORDS

The best vindaloo is prepared in mustard-oil... Beef and pork, or duck, can be made into this excellent curry. The following ingredients are employed in its preparation. Ghee, six chittacks*, lard or oil may be used; garlic ground, one tablespoon; garlic, bruised, one tablespoonful; ginger, ground, one tablespoonful; chillies, ground, two teaspoonful; coriander-seed, one teaspoonful; coriander-seed, roasted and ground, half a teaspoonful; bay leaves, or Tej-path, two or three; peppercorns, quarter-chittack; cloves, half a dozen roasted and ground; cardamoms, half a dozen roasted and ground; cinnamon, half a dozen sticks; vinegar, quarter-pint.

Take a ser*, of beef or pork, and cut it into large square pieces, and steep them in vinegar with slat and the ground condiments given above, for a whole night. Warm the Ghee, lard, or mustard-oil, with the ingredients in which it has been soaking over-night and add the meat with the peppercorns and bay leaves, and allow the whole to simmer slowly over a gentle fire for a couple of hours, or until the meat is quite tender. When preparing pork into vindaloo, omit the cloves, cardamoms and cinnamon.

WH Dawe, *The Wife's Help to Indian Cookery*, 1888
(**One chittack = roughly one ounce; one ser = about one kilogram*)

*The Cambridge rowing team's all-madras diet
had paid off handsomely.*

ORIGIN OF THE SPICES

Cinnamon

In European cookery, cinnamon is most often associated with puddings, sweets or desserts such as apple pie, mincemeat or rice pudding. In Mexico, it is used to flavour hot drinks and chocolate. In Morocco, it goes into the tagine pot (the traditional earthenware cooking pot with lid), helping to bridge the flavour gap between fruit and meat. In curry, it is used as a whole bark to add fragrance to rice and turns up ground in some curry powders – madras, for example – along with nutmeg to add sweet spice. Native to Sri Lanka, bushes tend to be a few feet high and shoots are regularly cropped to the ground after the curled inner bark is left to dry and peeled away. Pale brown, papery quills of cinnamon are the most highly prized. In ancient Egypt, cinnamon was worth more than gold and used in the embalming process, medicinally and to flavour drinks for those who could afford it. In the first century, Emperor Nero of Rome was said to have burnt a year's worth of cinnamon on his wife's funeral pyre – a signifier of both loss and wealth. The luxurious spice, and the promises of the riches that went with it, also lured the Portuguese and Dutch to Sri Lanka, where the latter set up a system of cultivation that still exists today. Today, no self-respecting cup of chai (Indian sweet tea) would be served without it.

BURNING QUESTIONS

Which of the following beers are not brewed in India?
a) Kingfisher
b) India Pale Ale
c) Belo
d) Cobra

Answer on page 151.

KEY INGREDIENTS OF A GREEN THAI CURRY

Many of these ingredients are, in fact, key ingredients of Thai cooking in general and give it the idiosyncratic flavour which has helped it over the past decade or two to gain an increasingly firm foothold within these previously unadventurous shores...

● **Apple and pea aubergines** (those small round unidentifiable green vegetables which are often the best bit)
● **Galangal** (*kha* in Thai. A relative of ginger, but more citrusy-tasting. It is ground up to form part of the base paste from which the curry is made. Aside from its use in cooking, it is mentioned by medieval saint Hildegard of Bingen as a remedy for deafness, while in Asia the pulped lime fruit is used as a remedy for dandruff)
● **Nam plah** (see the section on 'That Fish Sauce Stuff')
● **Kaffir lime leaves** (...also called makrut lime leaves. Unlike lemongrass, which is not the grass of lemons, these are actually the leaves of particular species of Asian lime. Some would say fresh new leaves from any citrus tree except orange are a reasonable replacement, but in any case, thanks to the popularity of Thai cooking it's not hard to get hold of the real thing now)
● **Lemongrass** (a handy herb indeed: the aromatic lemony smell of lemongrass, also called cochin or malabar grass, comes from a chemical called citral. Citral's also used as a flavouring for drinks, and as an ingredient in perfume. And lemongrass has long been used as an insect repellent, although the jury's out on how effective it is)
● **Green chillis** (to make a red curry, red chillis are used)
● **Thai basil** (for garnish)
● **Coconut milk/cream**
● **Strips of beef, chicken, prawns or vegetables...** whatever takes your fancy!

The curry is served in a bowl (the sauce is quite thin) with a separate bowl of rice. There are different kinds of Thai rice to choose from – coconut, jasmine, sticky – but many people find plain old steamed best to set off the curry.

Deciphering the curry house menu...

If curry is loosely defined as a saucy number, biryani is one of many dishes that fall short of the tag. Nevertheless, this celebratory rice dish (it is often served at Indian weddings) provides a tasty alternative to straight boiled rice as the main tool for soaking all that korma or vegetable curry up. Another chart-topping Mughlai number, biryani morphed from the Persian slow-cooked rice and meat dish pilaf, originally cooked by nomadic shepherds; the sixth-century caliphs in Baghdad simply refined it, using only the best rice. They also developed numerous versions, piled with fruits, nuts, saffron, raisins, onion and garlic, while some varied the colour of the rice in statements of wit, decoration and humour (hence the multi-coloured 'pilau' rice we know today). In Emperor Akbar's court (1555-1605), the delicately flavoured pilau met the pungent and spicy dishes of Hindustan to become biryani. Using Persian techniques, meat was marinated in yoghurt, onions, garlic, almonds and spices. This was then briefly fried before being transferred to a large pot. Partially cooked rice was heaped over, and saffron soaked in milk poured over to give aroma and flavour. Coals were then placed at the base and on the lid of the pot and the whole thing slow-cooked. Even today, biryani should be savoured for the time it takes to cook, and it is appreciated as such all over the world – if it's chicken fried rice you're after, head for the Chinese.

Heat factor: Blows hot and cold.

GET FIT WITH FENUGREEK

A popular ingredient in Indian curry pastes, pickles and Pakistani dahls, the seeds and leaves of the fenugreek plant are said to have some pretty interesting effects. For a start, the dried leaves have a strong characteristic scent, and a bitter taste, meaning that not only do they need to be used sparingly, they also have a somewhat smelly side effect on the eater's sweat and urine. This would normally be enough to put any self-conscious diner off consuming the spice; however, every negative has its positive equivalent; fenugreek is widely used as a milk-producing agent by nursing mothers, is used in India to condition hair, is used as a treatment for diabetes, is said to increase breast size, and is used by bodybuilders the world over to supplement their fitness regime.

Common herbs and spices used in Thai cuisine include:

Chilli
(*Phrik* in Thai)

Cumin
(*Yi-ra* in Thai)

Galangal
(*Kha* in Thai)

Garlic
(*Kra-thiam* in Thai)

Ginger
(*Khing* in Thai)

Hoary Basil
(*Maneg-lak* in Thai)

Kaffir
(*Ma-krut* in Thai), the leaves, peel
and juice of the kaffir lime

Lemongrass
(*Ta-khrai* in Thai)

Lime
(*Ma-nao* in Thai)

Marsh mint
(*Sa-ra-nae* in Thai)

Pepper
(*Phrik-Thai* in Thai)

Sacred basil
(*Ka-phrao* in Thai)

Shallot
(*Hom* in Thai)

Sweet basil
(*Ho-ra-pha* in Thai)

Turmeric
(*Khamin* in Thai)

The 'Kashmir'
In the words of that literary Raj, Rudyard Kipling,
some things are 'just so'...

The mind often boggles at why someone would name their curry house after a war-torn land between India and Pakistan. But those who have visited the region or tasted its food will gladly encourage you to pull up a pew at the local Kashmir – be it Bradford, Boston or Penang – and tuck in with relish. Sadly the area that lends its name to many a British curry house signage (gold and swirling italics seem to be *de rigeur* here) is now more known for its militant power struggles and its recent earthquake than for the beauty of its mountains, the generosity of its people, its fine pashminas or the finesse and legacy of its dishes. Mughal cuisine gained much from the combination of Persian cooking techniques with new ingredients such as ducks and vegetables from Kashmir. Today, when balti fans happily tuck into their favourite curry on a Friday night, little do they know that the dish is said to originate (by proxy of the pan it is cooked in) from the mountains of Baltistan, now a part of Pakistan-ruled Kashmir. The region is also responsible for the migration of the mutton and turnip shub deg – loosely meaning slow fire pot – that Lucknavis (those from Lucknow) still eat for breakfast today. If you want to make your visit to the Kashmir more authentic, do as the locals do: take along a little disc of 'ver' to crumble on your dish. This is a thin round piece of dried mustard, oil, garlic, chilli and spice paste, and is guaranteed to add some zing.

QUOTE UNQUOTE

Colouring does not enhance the flavour of the food, but a lot of people eat with their eyes. If consumers could become more aware of this, it would save restaurants feeling they will have to add the dye and be better for the health of the customer.
Chad Rahman, award-winning chef of Mumtaj, 115 London Road, St Albans, Hertfordshire, quoted in *Manchester Evening News*, 23 March 2004

COCKNEY SPICE

In Cockney rhyming slang, 'ginger' refers to homosexuals or homosexual behaviour – the original slang rhymed 'queer' with 'ginger beer'.

Garam masala (literally 'hot spice') is a powdered spice mix used throughout India as a flavour base for curries. Many different kinds exist, depending on the region of origin, but most forms contain a blend of the following spices:

Bay leaves
Black peppercorns
Cardamom
Cinnamon
Cloves
Cumin seeds
Fennel seeds
Fenugreek seeds
Mace
Nutmeg

CURRY WARS

Patak's in a pickle

On 24 March 2004, a raging family feud between members of Indian pickle giants Patak's ended in a provisional £12 million peace deal. Sisters Chitralekha Mehta and Anila Shastri claimed they had been cheated out of shares by their late father and founder of the empire, Laximishanker. They were each awarded a total of £6 million, although the deal could not be completed until details had been translated into Gujarati so that the family's 77-year-old matriarch, Shantagaury Pathak, could agree to the terms. The sisters claimed that 1,250 shares registered in their names in 1974 were unlawfully transferred to their brother Kirit in 1989. In turn he argued that the shares were registered as 'a matter of convenience' with the full knowledge that Hindu practice decreed that the family business could only be handed down to its sons. Kirit, with the full backing of his mother – a torchbearer for traditional affairs – accused the sisters of greed, gold-digging and opportunism, with Shantagaury calling them 'wicked'. However, Yogesh Pathak supported his sisters saying Kirit Pathak 'would make Machiavelli look like Mother Teresa'. In October 2004, the deal was reported as reneged, with lawyers John McDonnell QC and David Oliver QC entering into the argi-bhagi. Presiding judge Mr Justice Evans-Lombe refused to order a resumption of trial unless the sisters pursued a separate action against their brother. What a pickle!

34 *House number in George Street, London, where Dean Mahomet launched Britain's first Indian restaurant in 1809*

NUMBER OF INDIAN RESTAURANTS IN THE UK

Year	No of restaurants
1960	500
1970	1,200
1980	3,000
1990	5,100
1996	7,300
1997	7,600
2000	7,940
2001	8,432 (24% takeaway)
2004	8,750 (estimate)

(Source: www.menu2menu.com)

BURNING QUESTIONS

What do the following mean in Thai cuisine?
a) Sap
b) Sook
c) Yat sai
Answer on page 151.

A VERY WARM WELCOME, SIR...

The capital's very first curry houses
The Hindostanee Coffee House, 34 George Street,
Portman Square, London W1

The first commercial creation of curry powder was in 1780. This was preceded by the first appearance of a curry dish on a British menu at the Curry House in Norris Street, Haymarket. The first establishment to specialise in Indian cuisine, however, was Dean Mahomet's Hindostanee Coffee House. It received favourable reviews from the Epicure's Almanack when it opened in 1809, and was even advertised in *The Times*. But Mahomet's house 'for the Nobillity and Gentry where they might enjoy the Hookha with real Chilm tobacco and Indian dishes of the highest perfection', served up with colonial décor of bamboo chairs and Indian paintings proved a strain on his wallet. The Hooka Club – as nicknamed by one notorious patron, Charles Stewart (he was said to have had 16 Indian wives) – forced him into bankruptcy in 1812. From Patna, India, through Cork and London, Mahomet finally swapped spice for shampoo and opened a vapour house in Brighton, of which the Prince Regent (later crowned King George IV) foamed with praise.

The 'Taj Mahal'
In the words of that literary Raj, Rudyard Kipling,
some things are 'just so'...

The Taj Mahal is one of India's most famous buildings and represents the luxury and glamour that came with the rule of its fifth Mughal Emperor, Shah Jahan. As such, any curry house that takes this name also aspires to lure its customers through its doors with promises of riches within. A man with a penchant for high living and fine dining, Shah Jahan built his marble marvel at Agra (another popular curry house name) between 1631 and 1648 as a mausoleum for his wife, Arjumand Banu Begum.

He also built the beautiful city of Shahjahanabad, now known as Old Delhi, and commissioned Mughal artists to paint an exquisite series of miniatures known as the Padshahnama. According to Camellia Panjabi's book *50 Great Curries of India* (2000), Shah Jahan is also famous for concocting banquets consisting of dishes with only white sauces. For these he used white cumin, now referred to as *Shahi jeera* or 'royal cumin'.

Unfortunately, although his culinary passions were contagious and cook shops (perhaps India's first 'curry houses') did spring up in numerous bazaars, Shah Jahan's celebrity lifestyle was led at the expense of the Indian peasantry and his rule ended in a terrible famine. That didn't stop Sordar and Shomsor Bahadur opening Britain's first Taj Mahal restaurants in Brighton, Oxford and Northampton, all before World War II. Neither did it hinder more recent Taj Mahals in Dallas, South Africa or Prague. It should serve, however, as a warning to all those who are tempted to 'nip down the Taj' and overindulge...

WHO INVENTED THE BALTI?

A Brummie of course! It was invented on the Stratford Road in Birmingham in the 1970s as a meal for the workers going to and from the British Leyland factories. The factory has gone but the curry remains, which perhaps explains why there are so many curry houses in the city.

The dish is said to take its name from the thick steel pot in which the curry is both cooked and served, the Hindu and Bengali word for 'bucket'.

This curry was like a performance of Beethoven's Ninth Symphony that I'd once heard... especially the last movement, with everything screaming and banging 'Joy'. It stunned, it made one fear great art. My father could say nothing after the meal.

Anthony Burgess, English author, on his first curry, quoted in *Appetite For Murder: A Mystery-Lover's Cookbook*, by Kathy Borich

SPICE GUYS

Testimony from an early Spice Trail voyager

Beyond Mundus, sailing toward the east, after another two days' sail, or three, you reach Mosyllum, on a beach, with a bad anchorage. There are imported here the same things already mentioned, also silver plate, a very little iron, and glass. There are shipped from the place a great quantity of cinnamon, (so that this market-town requires ships of larger size), fragrant gums and spices.

Beyond this place, the coast trending toward the south, there is the Market and Cape of Spices, an abrupt promontory, at the very end of the Berber coast toward the east. The anchorage is dangerous at times from the ground-swell, because the place is exposed to the north. A sign of an approaching storm which is peculiar to the place, is that the deep water becomes more turbid and changes its colour. When this happens they all run to a large promontory called Tabae, which offers safe shelter.

Hippalus was the pilot who by observing the location of the ports and the conditions of the sea, first discovered how to lay his course straight across the ocean. For at the same time when with us the Etesian winds are blowing, on the shores of India the wind sets in from the ocean, and this southwest wind is called Hippalus, from the name of him who first discovered the passage across. From that time to the present day ships start, some direct from Cana, and some from the Cape of Spices; and those bound for Damirica throw the ship's head considerably off the wind; while those bound for Barygaza and Scythia keep along shore not more than three days and for the rest of the time hold the same course straight out to sea from that region, with a favorable wind, quite away from the land, and so sail outside past the aforesaid gulfs.

Anonymous (a merchant of the first century), *The Periplus of the Erythraean Sea: Travel and Trade in the Indian Ocean by a Merchant of the First Century*, 1912

The naan bread hat never really took off.

ORIGIN OF THE SPICES

Black Pepper

A native of southern India, the black pepper trade has always been prolific in the area and has found its place both in and on ancient Indian dishes, offspring curries and, in fact, nearly every form of modern cuisine in the world. Derived from the piperaceae family, the black pepper, *piper nigrum*, or *pippali* as it is known in Sanskrit, is actually bright red when fully mature. It can, however, produce white (dried minus the fruit) or green (often freeze-dried) pepper as well as the dried-out black peppercorns (composed of fruit and seed) and coarse ground version our table tops now know so well. Ancient texts reveal the pepper has been used in India since prehistoric times, but it was probably first cultivated on the shores of the Malabar Coast, now part of Kerala. As well as being a main component in food and Ayurvedic medicine, black pepper was also termed as 'black gold' and was used as a form of currency – the term 'peppercorn rent' still exists today. By way of ancient Greece and Rome, black pepper made its way from Indian shores to Europe, Egypt and further afield – Egypt's King Ramses II was even found with a corn up each nostril in his final resting place. Piperine (the chemical found in black pepper) may provide only 1% of the heat produced by the chilli pepper, but it still makes the world hot enough under the collar to make up around one fifth of today's current spice trade.

Manchester's 'Curry Mile' has over 20 curry houses. They are:

Al Bilal Restaurant

Al Nawaz

Andalos

Darbar Restaurant Indian Cuisine

Fizzler

Hanaan Restaurant

Jaffa Halal Mediterranean Restaurant

King Cobra Indian & Sri Lankian Cuisine

Kurdistan Restaurant Middle Eastern Cuisine

Lal Haweli

Lal Qila Indian Cuisine

Marmara

Mr Singh

Mughli Indian Cuisine

New Tabak Pakistani, Indian & Chinese Restaurant

Paradise Restaurant

Pink Garlic

Punjab Tandoori Restaurant

Royal Naz Indian Restaurant

Saki Turkish Bar & Grill

Sanam

Sangam Restaurant

Shaandaar Indian Cuisine

Shahenshah Tandoori

Shere Khan Indian Cuisine

Shezan

Shezan Restaurant & Take Away

Spicy Hut

A real biryani requires a high level of skill, because the marinated meat is covered with rice that is already two-thirds cooked. Then it is sealed and steamed so that the raw meat cooks in the same time as the rice. It needs a large quantity to work.
Vivek Singh, executive chef of the Cinnamon Club, Old Westminster Library, Great Smith Street, London, quoted in *The Observer Food Monthly*, 12 May 2002

IT'S IN THE DICTIONARY

Curry/Cur'ry/, *n.* [**Tamil kari.**] [Written also currie.]

1. (Cookery) A kind of sauce much used in India, containing garlic, pepper, ginger, and other strong spices.
2. A stew of fowl, fish, or game, cooked with curry.

Curry powder (**Cookery**), a condiment used for making curry, formed of various materials, including strong spices, as pepper, ginger, garlic, coriander seed, etc.

Curry/Cur'ry/, *v. t.*
To flavor or cook with curry.

Curry/Cur'ry/, *v. t.* [imp. & p. p. Curried (-r?d); p. pr. & vb. n. Currying.] [OE. curraien, curreien, OF. cunreer, correier, to prepare, arrange, furnish, curry (a horse), F. corroyer to curry (leather) (cf. OF. conrei, conroi, order, arrangement, LL. conredium); cor- (L. com-) + roi, rei, arrangement, order; prob. of German origin, and akin to E. ready. See Ready, Greith, and cf. Corody, Array.]

1. To dress or prepare for use by a process of scraping, cleansing, beating, smoothing, and coloring; -- said of leather.
2. To dress the hair or coat of (a horse, ox, or the like) with a currycomb and brush; to comb, as a horse, in order to make clean.
    Your short horse is soon curried.   *--Beau. & Fl.*
3. To beat or bruise; to drub; -- said of persons.
    I have seen him curry a fellow's carcass handsomely.
                                        --Beau. & Fl.
4. To curry favor, to seek to gain favor by flattery or attentions. *See Favor, n.*

Webster's Revised Unabridged Dictionary, 1913

---

40   *Thousands of pounds that was fined to Shere Khan restaurant, a Manchester curry house, after a customer found a live cockroach in his poppadums*

Recipe for curative Bengal stew, from *What to Tell the Cook; or The Native Cook's Assistant, Being a Choice Collection of Recipes for Indian Cookery, Pastry, &c, &c,* 1875.

$1/2$ teacup broth or gravy

1 dessertspoon anchovy sauce

1 dessertspoon ketchup or sauce

1 dessertspoon lime juice

$1/4$ teaspoon red pepper

$1/2$ teaspoon black pepper

1 teaspoon flour

1 teaspoon butter

1 large onion, boiled to a mash

1 dessertspoon sherry

Mix well, pour over a cold boiled fowl, skinned and cut to pieces, warm up slowly, and serve in a hot dish.

CURRIED WORDS

I don't like curry ready-meals and curry sauces. The thing is, the further they get away from the right way to make it, the worse they get it seems to me. And the right way to make it is for intimate cooking and grinding of the spices, you know intimate contact with heat in the pan with relatively small quantities. But unfortunately the big manufacturers do it in 5,000 litre vats and give it, you know, 10 seconds for the spices to cook and then pile in the next load of ingredients. So you get that, oh I don't know, that raw taste.

The other thing I get increasingly, what's the word? Observant about (lets not be emotive) is the addition of additives like acetic acid, preservatives and stabilisers. And 'use by' dates on things like, say, mango chutney which simply doesn't need it. I've just finished a jar of 15-year-old chilli pickle that was in a huge two litre jar which came from India and doesn't have any preservatives and, of course, would have lasted for considerably longer. That's where I think the journalists should be concentrating their efforts – in the factories. Not on what the restaurants are doing which is passable and very good in some cases whether it's authentic or not.

Pat Chapman, from an interview on curryhouse.co.uk

HOW TO CURRY FAVOUR

Win awards at your local curry house for pronouncing the dishes correctly. You might even get an extra 'pappa-dum' or two...

Chapatti	cha-pat-ee
Dahl	dahl
Ghee	sound the g as in 'good'
Kebabs	ke-bhabs
Lychees	lie-cheese
Maldive	last syllable rhymes with 'give'
Pakoras	pa-kor-ras
Panthay kaukswe	pan-thay cow-sway
Parathas	per-ra-tas
Pilau	pill-ow (as in 'cow')
Poppadums	pappa-dums
Raita	rye-ta
Sambal	sam-bhal (Indian)
Sambol	sam-boll (Ceylonese)
Vindaloo	vin-dah-loo

THE MAN WITH THE CURRY TOUCH

James Bond is famous for his drinking habits, but have you ever seen him eat? While food references are few and far between in 007's scenes, curry comes up trumps when it does get a look in – although it's not always on the winning team. Bond's third appearance in 1964 saw him pitted against Goldfinger (in the film of the same name), a man with a bit of an obsession for the yellow stuff. The golden-haired, golden-suited villain not only had a taste for golden girls – not even the dazzling Pussy Galore could satisfy his cravings. In Ian Fleming's novel, Goldfinger is said to eat and drink gold, namely cheese soufflé and curry – clearly bright yellow by these Technicolor times – washed down with some glowing Goldtropfchen wine. It's not clear if Goldfinger ate the colourific curry with his hands, but his 'golden' finger could warn that you can become what you eat.

Curry also plays a starring role in the 1983 blockbuster, *Octopussy*, when Bond hands a wad of Indian cash to his accomplice with an outrageous: 'That should keep you in curry for a few weeks'. While the tuk-tuk chase inspired the name for a chain of curry houses from Glasgow to Torquay and Swansea, it appears curry's reputation – and associations – hadn't moved on much in 20 years. Today Bond fans can mix crime-busting with a Thai curry on Thailand's Koh Ping-Gan Island, rechristened 'James Bond Island' after *The Man with the Golden Gun* was shot there.

FLOCK-PAPER FAVOURITES: PASANDA

Deciphering the curry house menu...

A variation on the Hindi word *pasande* meaning 'favourite one', the 'korma with a crunch' actually refers to the prime cut of meat used in this north Indian dish. Served in the court of the Mughal Emperors, it was originally made with a prize leg of lamb that had been flattened into strips, marinated in yoghurt and chilli powder and fried in a dish with numerous spices (cumin, peppercorn, cardamom, garlic and garam masala). To become a pasanda the meat is then placed in a saucepan with onions, coriander, chillis and sometimes cinnamon and black pepper. Another mild dish on the British curry house menu, it often includes the addition of cream, coconut milk, pureed tomatoes and cashew nuts or almonds – the 'badam' of a badam pasanda and now one of the more associated ingredients – to make it even more universally palatable. Indeed Patak's Pasanda Almond and Yoghurt Sauce is even labelled as 'ideal for all the family' – a family favourite perhaps...

Heat factor: Mild and mellow.

QUOTE UNQUOTE

The French intelligence, fine and keen as it is, does not penetrate the depths of curry lore.
Royal consort Prince Albert Saxe-Coburg, as quoted in *Curry: The Story of the Nation's Favourite Dish* (2003), by Shrabani Basu

---

CURRIED WORDS

On the devotional aspects of Brahmin eating habits

They give out publicly that the gods command certain offerings to be made to their temples, which offerings are simply the things that the Brahmins themselves wish for, for their own maintenance and that of their wives, children, and servants. Thus they make the poor folk believe that the images of their gods eat and drink, dine and sup like men, and some devout persons are found who really offer to the idol twice a day, before dinner and supper, a certain sum of money. The Brahmins eat sumptuous meals to the sound of drums, and make the ignorant believe that the gods are banqueting.

St Francis Xavier, *Letters From India, to the Society of Jesus at Rome*, 1543

*'Look!' said Marjorie to her startled husband,
'your curry has corroded my plate!'*

YOU CAN CURRY LOVE

Want to spice up your love life? Try curry. Key ingredients, ginger, nutmeg, clove and pepper all appeared in the *Karma Sutra* as ancient love aids. Jack Turner's *Spice – The History of Temptation* (2004) tells of eleventh-century sexologist Constantine suggesting an: 'electuary of ginger, pepper, galangal, cinnamon and various herbs', after lunch and dinner, as a latter day Viagra. Traders were lured across the oceans in search of their hot properties. Later Tennyson, Shakespeare and Marlowe waxed lyrical about recipes for love from the exotic East. Today, in the run up to St Valentine's Day, getting 'sex on your plate' is always big news, with curry, oysters and avocados consistently hailed as ways to 'spice up the night'. Unfortunately, urban myth supported by a handful of salubrious studies, claims that guys 'are what they eat' – making garlic, onion or over-spiced curries not great choices for a tasteful night. Adding sweet coconut milk might be the answer, with some sources suggesting a romantic Thai green curry as the perfect dish. Extreme curry lovers who can't get enough of the stuff, can go all the way safely with some curry-flavoured condoms (yes, they do exist apparently) and a vindaloo for two.

44 *Year in the nineteenth century when celebrated English cook, Mrs Turnbull, wrote her curry powder recipe*

MAKE YOUR OWN CURRY POWDER

It may be much simpler to buy a pre-prepared curry mixture, but
some traditionalists like to start from scratch

Ingredients:
2 teaspoons mustard seed
1 teaspoon fenugreek or 2 teaspoons celery seed
4 tablespoons ground coriander
4 teaspoons ground cumin
4 teaspoons turmeric
2 teaspoons ground cardamom
2 teaspoons mace
1 teaspoon cinnamon
1 teaspoon fresh ground pepper
$1/_2$ tsp. each: cayenne, ground ginger, ground cloves, nutmeg

Method:
Briefly roast mustard and fenugreek seeds, allow them to cool and
then grind to a powder with a mortar and pestle. Gently combine
the powder with the remaining ingredients.

WHAT IS BEAN CURD?

You've probably seen it on your local takeaway menu, you just can't
get away from bean curd (tofu) in a Thai, Chinese or Japanese
restaurant. So what is it and where does it come from?

Tofu is actually Chinese in origin (where it is also, and more
correctly, referred to as 'doufu'). It is made from coagulating soy
milk, which is pressed into blocks, rather like the way in which
cheese is manufactured. In south-east Asia, tofu comes in many
forms: fresh, fried, dried, processed, fermented and flavoured
(including sweet and savoury variations for dessert). It is also frozen
and layered in Japanese cuisine, and made from other forms of bean,
including chickpeas and black beans. But when it comes to curry,
you're most likely to see it sautéed and then added to a Thai red or
green curry to soften the spice.

It's also a popular health-giving ingredient. Soy isoflavones are said
to help your body fight against cancer, and reduce signs of the
menopause (particularly hot flushes) in women of a certain age. It is
also high in protein and very low in fat (unless fried), which is good
news for anyone not on the Atkins diet.

A CURRY CLASSIC

**Recipe for make-it-yourself classic madras curry sauce,
in English (and Tamil, just in case)...**

1lb coriander seed (*Dummiah*)
¼lb turmeric (*Huldee*)
¼lb red chillis (*Lal mirchee*)
¼lb black pepper (*Kala mirchee*)
¼lb mustard seed (*Rai*)
2oz dry ginger (*Souat*)
2oz garlic (*Lussum*)
2oz vendinne
½lb salt (*Nimmuck*)
½lb sugar (*Shuggeo*)
2oz cumin seed (*Zeera*)
½lb gram (*Chenna*)

Fry the gram and take off the husks, then pound it with the
other ingredients and mix with

½ pint salad oil
½ pint vinegar

A TIFF-IN THE HOUSE

On 16 May 2006, the Taj Mahal in Haverfordwest was one of just 14 restaurants competing in the inaugural Tiffin Cup (over 40 curry houses participated in the heats), a national curry cook-off launched by MPs Michael Fabricant, John Barrett and Keith Vaz to celebrate south Asian cuisine. Nominated by jalfrezi-loving local MP Stephen Crabb and his constituents, the Pembrokeshire favourite, which opened in 1979, specialises in Bangladeshi and Indian subcontinent cuisine. Judges were presenters Loyd Grossman, Ainsley Harriott and Nina Wadia from the TV sitcom *Goodness Gracious Me* with contestants enticed by the promise of a year's supply of Cobra beer – and of course the very first Tiffin Cup. It obviously worked for proud prize-winner, the chef of the Taj Mahal, who not only brought culinary excellence to the Houses of Parliament, but also his very own pots, pans and uniform. Manager Abul Hussein, the chef's brother, did admit to some nerves, although he now has more pressing things on his mind: how to prepare enough chicken bhuna (the restaurant's most popular dish) to cope with the tirade of Tiffin Cup-savvy customers the new prestige is set to bring.

---

46 *Percentage, according to 2003 figures, of the world's spice exports accounted for by India*

TIKKA-ED TRAIN FARE

India's railway system was initiated by the British in 1857 – albeit to help transport their own troops around the country. Travel on an Indian train today and your dining experience will be much the same as back in the day. Wherever the train stops, hawkers will be waiting to offer you their fare – whether it be curry, salad, bread or rice. On some trains, attendants even pass down the train regularly with standard foil parcels of the same. On the Rajdhani Express and the Shatabdi Express (two major intercity links) dinner comes part and parcel of the fare and food is served at your seat. Thankfully India's railway food has stopped trying to appease British tastes with curry cutlets (leftover meat or vegetables, curried and shaped like a lamb chop with a mock bone stuck in) left off the menu. At the top end of train fare, passengers on the Orient Express can enjoy many of Asia's dishes while on board – fricassee of asparagus in a delicate Thai curry bouillon for brunch and Malaysian nonya curry for dinner are highlights of one Asian voyage.

Back in Britain, curry shows up on our trains as ready meals, chicken tikka sandwiches or curried chips. When a GNER buffet car once ran out of food in 2002, one hungry passenger wasn't to be defeated. Deko Primo simply ordered ahead to an Indian takeaway in Peterborough and had a curry waiting when the train drew up at the platform.

BURNING QUESTIONS

What do the following mean in Thai cuisine?
a) Dip
b) Haeng
c) Pat
Answer on page 151.

CURRIED THINKING

Mullaga-tawny signifies Pepper Water. The progress of the inexperienced peripatetic Palaticians has lately been arrested by those outlandish words being pasted on the windows of our Coffee Houses; it has we believe answered the 'restaurateur's purpose' and often excited JOHN BULL to walk in and taste: – the more familiar name of Curry Soup – would, perhaps, not have had any sufficient of the charms of novelty to seduce him from his much-loved MOCK TURTLE. It is a fashionable soup and a great favourite with our East Indian friends.
Dr William Kitchiner, *The Cook's Oracle*, 1829

The capital's very first curry houses
The Shafi, Gerard Street, London WC2

At the turn of the nineteenth century, Lascars – Asian seamen recruited by the East India Company – often jumped ship in Britain when hideous seafaring conditions proved too much. Communities of them sprung up around the capital, and meeting places dished up curry as way of comfort and support. Salut e Hind – London's first recorded Indian 'restaurant' (the term for a collective place to eat, itself in a state of evolution) – was born in Holborn in 1911. But failing to influence, it left a gap for Mohammed Wayseem and Mohammed Rahim to try their hand; they opened The Shafi nearly 10 years later in 1920. Employing a number of Indian ex-seamen on its staff, it attracted like with like and became a popular Lascar hub and Indian Student Centre (by 1931, London's Indian student population was around 1,800). It was eventually taken over by Dharam Lal Bodua, run by an English manager, and employed a chain of Indian seamen chefs who would help the curry house phenomenon to spore and grow.

ORIGIN OF THE SPICES

Cardamom

After the vanilla pod, cardamom – a relative of the ginger family – with small black sticky seeds in a green pod, is the most expensive spice in the world market. The classic form originates from India's Malabar Coast (now in the region of Kerala), the forests of the Western Ghats (India's central mountainous area) and Ceylon (now Sri Lanka). However, variations grow throughout Guatemala, Asia and Indochina – the Krâvanh Mountains of Thailand and Cambodia were once termed the 'Cardamom Mountains' due to the excessive amount of the spice that grew there (in fact, the cardamom was of a 'false' variety, although still from the same ginger family).

The Greek word *kardamomon* gave the seed its current name – 'kard' meaning 'bitter stem' and 'amomon' meaning spice, derived from an Eastern word transported back with Alexander the Great. An ancient spice in various parts of the world, cardamom is known to have been adored by Scandinavian Vikings, used by the Egyptians as toothpaste and due to its camphorous-eucalyptine aroma, by the Greeks and Romans as a perfume – not an indication that cardamom-rich curry should make its way into the bathroom. It does however impart a warm and fresh flavour to Indian pilau rice, desserts and sweetmeats, tea and curry powder.

Singha beer – The classic Thai beer. Singha is Sanskrit for lion, and it's certainly the king of beers in the country. Other Asian beers found in the company of Thai food include Tiger (Singapore) and Kirin Ichiban (Japan).

Thai tea/coffee – South-east Asians are keen on sweet drinks and desserts, and condensed milk is a popular ingredient. It's used liberally in Thai tea and coffee, so if you order it, be prepared.

Coconut water – The milk from a very young coconut, coconut water is said to be good for the stomach and digestion, which may be just what you need after a particularly spicy jungle curry.

Lemongrass martini – This is not, strictly speaking, a Thai drink, but it incorporates one of the staple ingredients of Thai food. It's a common find in cocktail bars these days, although if you want to eat it with curry, you may have to make both at home.

Rice wine – There used to be a law in Thailand preventing the manufacture of rice wine on private premises. But a few years ago, for reasons best known to

themselves, the Thai government abolished the law – a decision which led to a proliferation of small producers. It's made, very simply, from rice, water and yeast, but it has to be drunk shortly after it's ready because unlike its Japanese cousin sake, it doesn't keep very well.

Palm wine – Palm trees are used for all sorts of things in Asia and Africa – oil, resin and sugar (jaggery) among them. Two of the region's most popular nuts, the coconut and the betel, come from palms. And palm toddy, or wine, is a popular, if somewhat acquired, taste. It's made from the sap of certain kinds of palm which is allowed, as with rice wine, to ferment.

Fruit juice – Not just your ordinary tropical fruit like mango or papaya, but longan, guava, tamarind, rambutan, dragon fruit – there are lots of interesting south-east Asian fruits which you may not have tried before. Rice wine is sometimes mixed with juice to give it flavour.

Diesel from a jerry can – (they said it was palm wine, but I'm still not sure...)

MRS BEETON'S CURRY WISDOM

Curried Veal

Ingredients: 2 slices of large cod, or the remains of any cold fish; 3oz of butter, 1 onion sliced, a teacupful of white stock, thickening of butter and flour, 1 small teaspoonful of curry-powder, ¼ pint of cream, salt and cayenne to taste.

Mode: Flake the fish, and fry it of a nice brown colour with the butter and onions; put this in a stewpan, add the stock and thickening, and simmer for 10 minutes. Stir the curry-powder into the cream; put it, with the seasoning, to the other ingredients; give one boil, and serve.

Time – ¾ hour.

Average cost – with fresh fish, 3s.

Seasonable – from November to March.

Sufficient for – 4 persons.

Isabella Beeton – aka 'Mrs Beeton',
Book of Household Management, 1861

QUOTE UNQUOTE

To me the word 'curry' is as degrading to India's great cuisine as the term 'chop suey' was to China's. If 'curry' is an oversimplified name for an ancient cuisine, then 'curry powder' attempts to oversimplify (and destroy) the cuisine itself.
Madhur Jaffrey, Indian-born actress, TV presenter and writer

CURRIED HORSE ANYONE?

Why curry favour? It's an expression bandied about for all manner of reasons, but none of them has anything to do with curry – the food that is. To curry favour is interpreted as seeking to get into someone's good books. The curry in this case is the horse-riding term for grooming or rubbing down the animal – hence the curry comb (also nothing to do with food and best left well out of the kitchen). The phrase 'a short horse is easily curried' certainly does not mean he makes a better vindaloo. Some etymologists say that 'favour' derives from the word 'Favel', a half-man, half-horse character from a fourteenth-century French satirical novel. The horse-man in question was not known for his virtuous side and getting on the wrong side of this evil beast was certainly not advised. On the other hand, give Favel a good currying and he could be persuaded to not kick up a fuss.

CURRY WORLD

**Curry collectors unite and feed that spicy fetish on eBay.
On 21 June 2006, you could buy…**

	£bid	£p&p
50g Lobo green curry paste – bb15.05.2008	2.23	0.79
You Cannot Die – Ian Curry – Incredible research on death	0.99	2.40
The Worst Witch (the movie), starring Diana Rigg, Tim Curry *New*	8.75	1.95
Slimming World's Curry Feast	6.00	2.00
100g 10mm boiles, curry, chocolate, strawberry and more	0.99	0.80
Indian spice, extra hot chilli powder (use for curry)	0.60	0.50
Stainless steel balti 6, Indian cooking set	4.99	5.99
Wayfarer camping curry pack (veg curry)	4.95	free
Small rubber curry comb	0.55	free

TALES OF THE CAMPFIRE

Long journeys across India were often part and parcel of those who were employed to maintain colonial rule. Their long-suffering other halves were often required to do the same. In 1864, making curry along the way seemed to be a prerequisite. In *The Englishwoman in India: Containing Information for the Use of Ladies Proceeding To, or Residing In, The East Indes* (1864) by A Lady Resident, the anonymous lady includes a list of ingredients for a 'long march across India'. She deems milk, eggs, kids, fowls, onions and chillis as 'items you can always depend upon procuring'. She goes on to say that tea, coffee, sugar and biscuits must be brought along. Pepper, salt, gingerbread nuts, sago and arrowroot are essentials; as are table rice, fine flour and potatoes. A few tins of preserves such as peas, carrots or mock-turtle soup can really go a long way; plus a tin of bacon, a piece of salted beef and some tongues. Last of all, the trip wouldn't be complete without bread, jam, pickles, chutney, sauce, and last but not least, curry powder. Look closely and you can almost see, nay smell, that pot of nineteenth-century, Anglo-Indian, classic campsite curry on the boil…

GOING OUT FOR AN ENGLISH

In an English restaurant in India. Ordering some food...

Indian man one: For starter we shall have six... no, 12 bread rolls. For main course everybody?
Indian man two: What's the blandest thing on the menu?
James the waiter: The scampi's our specialty, sir.
Indian man two: I'll have that.

This scene, from the 1998 hit Asian skit show *Goodness Gracious Me* (named after a song performed by Peter Sellers as a cod-Indian and Sophia Loren to promote the 1960 film *The Millionairess*), is one of the most memorable – namely because the parody rings so true. A group of Bombay youths out for an English after a few beers, mispronounce the waiter's name, order the blandest thing on the menu (one opts for the safe option of a curry) and demand 24 portions of chips. Although similar jokes had been played out by Billy Connolly and Rowan Atkinson (as a hilarious Indian waiter in his 'Guys After the Game' sketch), this turn around of events really hit home with its audience. Getting tanked up and going down the Indian and ordering 24 poppadums and the hottest thing on the menu – usually a vindaloo – would never be the same again.

CURRY CRIMES

A very bitter end

There you are, looking forward to tucking into your favourite tucker of spicy curry and what happens? You wake up dead. Such was the fateful end of one Julian Webb, who was poisoned to death by Dena Thompson one dark night in West Sussex, newspapers reported. Webb's mother Rosemary, never believed her son had taken his own life and had in fact warned him against the marriage following an unfeasible whirlwind romance. Rosemary's intuition was proven to be spot on: since Webb's death, Dena had in fact been on a decade-long sexual, financial and physical rampage worthy of any black widow. It was only after she was cleared of trying to kill her third husband Richard Thompson (the court heard she attacked him with a baseball bat and knife after allegedly fearing for her life during a bondage session) that Webb's body was exhumed in 2000. It turns out that Dena bigamously wed Webb for his £36,000 death benefit and then tried to con Thompson and two former lovers out of £12,000. 'The men of Britain can sleep safe tonight knowing she has been taken off the streets,' proclaimed detective chief inspector Martyn Underhill after she was successfully prosecuted for murder in 2003.

BURNING QUESTIONS

Ghee is often used in Indian and Pakistani cuisine, but what is it?
Answer on page 151.

BOX OFFICE HOTS

Films inspired by curry, if not in taste, then at least in name...

Kare raisu (*Curry Rice*), 1962

Ga li la jiao (*Curry and Pepper*), 1990

Dr Curry, 1996

Cheap Curry and Calculus, 1996

Die Curry Insel, 1999

No Worry Chicken Curry, 2000

Jesus the Curry King, 2002

Curry Cookies, 2004

French Fries and Curry, 2004

One Dollar Curry, 2004

GLOBAL WARMING: JAPAN

On the spice trail and around the world on the good ship Curry...

Very few ancient or colonial enlisted Indians got as far as Japan – and even today the proportion of Indians who live there is relatively few – so how did curry become such a huge national dish? One theory goes that 'curry' found its way there via Shanghai, possibly as a way to reintroduce iron-rich red meat into the diet with nouveau dishes such as beef curry (in the nineteenth century, the nation was apparently trying to find ways to make their population taller and stronger).

What is known is that the first commercial curry powders were being made in Osaka by 1903. The first curry may, in fact, have been presented at the International Competition of 1863, alongside rice, sliced chillis and a thick sauce. Japanese preserves – fukujinzuke – are now a regular side dish to curried meals. Popular curries include keema curry – made with minced beef, often with peas – and steamed and lightly fried curry-stuffed buns. Making curries at home is also widely encouraged with chocolate-like blocks of curry roux, which melt in the pan to make an instant sauce. Simply add to the pre-packaged setto (family-sized) of curray-yo (curry ingredients) and you're off.

In India, paan wallahs (hawkers of the Dracula-like digestive betel leaf) compete with chai wallahs to provide an *après* curry experience for the nation's diners. You don't have to go to India these days to experience the hot, sweet, milky tea that is traditionally served out in its streets and on its trains. Now famous as one of India's 'traditional' drinks, in fact chai, like curry, is a relatively new concept and is another Anglo-Indian affair. Traders brought tea to India from China – contrary to popular belief, tea as a drink does not originate there, although a similar tea leaf was eventually found in Indian Assam – and it was the colonial British Tea Association and a pushy marketing campaign that helped make tea one of the nation's favourite drinks. Of course, the Indians added a spicy twist to make it their own. The most common spices used in a chai masala are cardamom, cinnamon, ginger, cloves and pepper. Lots of sweetened milk is *de rigeur* making it hard to resist a second cup. By the time you're ready to move on, your curry should be well and truly on its way down. Aptly, 'chai pani' is a phrase that denotes the offering of hospitality on the subcontinent.

THE CULINARY ADVENTURES
OF DEAN MAHOMET

Letter XVIII: *On entering the bustling Hindu territory of Benaras, on the north side of the Ganges, after leaving Denaphore in 1775...*

'The native Indians, or Hindoos, are men of strong natural genius, and are, by no means, unacquainted with literature and science, as the translation of the Ayeen Akberry [Ain-i Akbari] into English, has fully evinced... The women in general, except in the higher scenes of life, prepare the food for their husbands and families; as no Hindoo would make use of any but what his wife dresses for him: it consists chiefly of rice, fish, and vegetables, well seasoned with pepper and other spices, to which they add pickles of various sorts. The men, who always eat together, unaccompanied by the women, previously take off their turbans, shoes, and outside garments, and wash before and after meals. They afterwards withdraw to another apartment, where they enjoy themselves with smoking tobacco and chewing betel. They use no spirits or other liquors, but are particularly nice in the taste of different waters, and consider their choice of them a great luxury.'

Dean Mahomet, *The Travels of Dean Mahomet*, 1794

54 *Year in the thirteenth century which Marco Polo was born, who opened up the spice route in his expedition in 1271*

QUOTE UNQUOTE

Books about curries… are published continually, with the success of a well-ticking clock. Special restaurants all over the world serve nothing but curries. Spice merchants grow rich on making their regional and private blends of curry powder. In other words, reputations can and do depend upon the authenticity of the recipe first and then of the powder that goes with the sauce, the skill with which the sauce is made, and in many cases the atmosphere in which the whole is served.
MFK Fisher, US gastronome

MAKE YOUR OWN McTIKKA (KIND OF)

A very, very, very quick recipe for curried hamburgers, for curry lovers who be tempted to leave their pride at the golden gates.

One pack minced beef or lamb
Half a bag of split peas
Knob of ghee or butter
Dollop of green masala paste (fresh green herbs
such as parsley, coriander and mint)
Smattering of flour

Mix together. Shape into burgers. Roll in flour. Heat oil in pan. Gently brown until cooked. Serve in pitta bread with yoghurt. Eat. Pat stomach. Smile.

TV DINNERS

The setting: Lillicrap Ltd, makers of seaside novelties. The date: 21 November to 26 December 1969. The cast: Eric Sykes, Spike Milligan, Norman Rossington and Kenny Lynch. The script: Johnny Speight of *Till Death Do Us Part* fame. Despite its concrete cast, London Weekend Television aired a total of six episodes of *Curry and Chips* before it was cancelled. The show revolved around an Irish-Pakistani factory worker, Kevin O'Grady – a 'blacked'-up, ridiculously accented Spike Milligan (reminiscent of Peter Sellers in *The Party*) who also helped come up with the idea – and the racial tension between him and his bigoted white co-workers. As vitriolic as the hottest vindaloo, a blatantly racist script left viewers reeling, indigestible even in its satire; worryingly, some were said to delight in the comments – a sign, perhaps, of the times. In the case of this particular TV dinner, curry and chips didn't sit well side by side.

WHOSE RECIPE DID YOU SAY IT WAS?

Black Caps. Take out the cores, and cut into halves twelve large apples. Place them on a tin patty-pan as closely as they can lie, with the flat side downward. Squeeze a lemon into two spoonfuls of orange-flower water, and pour it over them. Shred some lemon-peel fine, and throw over them, and grate fine sugar over all. Set them in a quick oven, and half an hour will do them. Throw fine sugar all over the dish, when you send them to table.

The first English cookery book to contain a recipe for curry was Hannah Glasse's *Art of Cookery*, first published in 1747. However, her recipe soon appeared elsewhere. The example above comes from John Farley's *The London Art of Cookery*, in which he is said to have lifted more than one recipe from Glasse. But then she was pretty prone to a spot of lifting herself. She is said to have taken her recipe for curry from *The Whole Duty of a Woman*, first published in 1737, which was itself said to have been a collection of stolen recipes that pillaged John Middleton's *Five Hundred New Recipes in Cookery* (1734) who in turn apparently copied it from John Nott's *Cook's and Confectioner's Dictionary* (1726).

WHAT'S SO GREAT ABOUT GINGER?

King Henry VIII encouraged the use of ginger to protect England from the plague and Pythagoras swore by it in Ancient Greece. It seems that ginger has always been renowned for its healing powers, but why and should you really believe the hype? We trawled for the latest advice on the internet, and learned that:

In 2005, the American Phytotherapy Research Laboratory in Salt Lake City conducted a study on motion sickness, which proved that the testers who ate ginger could stand a full six minutes of spinning, compared to four and a half minutes for those testers who did not eat ginger.

Certain researchers in Japan believe that ginger contains a substance which can block a body's reflex to be sick, while their counterparts in Denmark believe that the spice can stop inflammation of blood vessels in the brain leading to migraine.

Ginger tea is also prescribed to relieve arthritis and according to research at Cornell University Medical College can help lower high cholesterol levels.

Miles was determined that the after-effects of vindaloo wouldn't spoil his clothing.

ORIGIN OF THE SPICES

Fenugreek

Fenugreek, or *methi*, as it is called in Hindi, is an important ingredient in many curries from dopiazas to vindaloos. It is, however, the least well-known spice in the West, where it has not traditionally been used as a culinary device. In tea or vitamin form, it is also used as an aid to breastfeeding, increasing lactation, as a device to aid menstrual pain and lower blood sugar, fenugreek has also been used as an insect repellent, weight gain aid in Libya and to produce a yellow dye. The name fenugreek actually stems from its use as hay fodder in ancient times – the Latin *foenum graenum* translates as 'Greek hay'. Both leaves and seeds are used in traditional curry cooking, where the plant is indigenous to India. Used well and in proportion, the strong, bitter aroma of the podded yellow seeds, when heated, impart a distinctive 'curry' taste and aroma, while the iron-rich leaves lend a milder flavour to hot dishes and salads. Thrown in carelessly, the nose and tastebuds can recoil. Heed the chef's warning – it is not advisable to curry up creamy kormas or tikka masalas with the stuff.

The 'Groover from Vancouver' (strictly Ontario, but well, we won't niggle over facts) – Bryan Adams – was not only something of a celebrity vegan over the years, he's something of a curry fan, too. An interview with *The Hindustan Times*, January 2006, heard Adams raving about India, saying he had 'dreamt about it as a boy'. Although he had not tried his hand at cooking it, he did get a real taste of heaven the following month, when in Mumbai for a show. English and Portuguese editor of his Turkish fan site www.bryanadams.org (it seems Adams has infiltrated the world more than curry), Mangelardo Ana Carolina wrote that the crooner was treated to some pre-concert spicy cuisine by executive chef of the Taj Lands End Hotel. The catering was of course Indian vegan, but the singer left the creation of the menu to Jitendra and his staff. Now well versed in that catchy ancient mantra 'Everything I do, I do it for you', the restaurant went all out to offer Adams an authentic welcome with home-grown organic vegetables from all over the country for his curries, organic flour for his rotis and tandoori breads, and a décor of fresh flowers and divas worthy of the 'Summer of 69'. While Indian classical music was playing during the actual meal, the excited chef was said to have been listening to Adams' music for five days flat. A later report by the *Indian Times* cited Bryan Adams as '...having his own Indian cook'. Presumably so he doesn't have to 'Drive All Night' to get a biryani.

GLOBAL WARMING: MYANMAR

On the spice trail and around the world on the good ship Curry...

Lodged between India and Thailand lies the controversial land of Myanmar – formerly Burma – nicknamed 'Land of the Golden Pagodas'. From India came Buddhism; Indian traders also brought many ingredients, including spice with them. When the British moved in and established Rangoon (now Yangon) as their capital, Indian workers went with them. Soon, half of the capital was deemed to be Indian, a dominating proportion. World War II and the Japanese occupation changed matters again and most Indians left, never to return in the wake of Burmese independence. The food, however, lived on and 'curry' with rice and noodles is now common currency on the streets of Myanmar. Curry powder is sometimes used but lemongrass and ngapi – fermented fish or shrimp sauce – makes things typically Burmese. One famous dish is the kala aw, 'a dish so hot that it would make an Indian scream': the word 'kala' is a derogatory reference to the 'black' skin of the Indians.

QUOTE UNQUOTE

We have evidence to suggest this is a national problem... and we are urging trading standards services across the UK to work with Indian restaurants in their area to ensure the amount of colorants used is within the legal limits.
Phil Thomas, food spokesman for the Trading Standards Institute, on the use of artificial colours in British curry houses in 2004

GOOD MORNING, BRITISH INDIA

Ingredients for curried balls. Boot-camp breakfast as recommended by the *Indian Military Manual of Cooking and Dietary* (1940): 'Published by authority of the commander-in-chief in India for the guidance of officers and others concerned with the messing of British troops in India.' Feeds 100 men:

25lb meat
8lb bread
6lb onions
1lb curry powder
1lb dripping
3lb flour
2oz salt
1oz pepper

Serve with manual motto: 'Pleasant flavours are desirable in diets. The average man cannot be nourished on tasteless food.'

CURRY – THE NATION'S FAVOURITE DISH?

Triggered by a 'what do people eat' survey conducted in 1999 by indigestion company Bi-so-dol, curry came up trumps in the takeaway category with 18% of the vote. Fish and chips – a precluded favourite – came a close second at 16% and pizza third. Tabloid interpretation omitted the takeaway slant and branded curry Britain's 'favourite dish'. In a run up speech to 2002 party political elections, resident foreign minister of the time, Robin Cook, deemed chicken tikka masala the 'nation's favourite dish' – an attempt perhaps to curry favour with the Asian communities in Britain. The papers had a field day, sparking nation-wide disputes about the credibility of curry as a true representative of our tastes – and indeed what curry actually was. In fact, Cook's comments only added fuel to the fire and curry – namely chicken tikka masala – is now firmly instilled as one of our favourite dishes of the day.

Restaurants on Manchester's famous 'Curry Mile' that have a BYOB (bring your own bottle) policy

Al Nawaz • Cinnamon • Darbar
Dildar • Hanaan • Lal Haweli
Lal Qila • Punjab • Royal Naz
Sangam • Shezan • Tabak

THAI CURRIES WHICH ARE NOT GREEN CURRY

There are many of us who, as soon as we set foot in a Thai restaurant, are set upon by opposing but equally powerful forces: the desire to try something a bit different, and the primal urge to order a green curry. Not totally equal forces... most diners, given enough time to think about it, will be pulled inexorably toward the dark side. So to give those rendangs and tom yums vying for a little bit of loving attention their chance in the limelight, here is a selection of Thai Curries Which Are Not Green Curry:

Red curry – OK, it's obvious, but it's still not green curry. One would expect red curry to be hotter because it's red, and it is. It is, apart from that, not hugely different to its verdant cousin.

Rendang – There are many cross-pollinations in south-east Asian cooking, and rendang is an example of the Indonesian influence in Thai cuisine. It incorporates many of the flavours familiar from Thai curries – lemongrass, galangal, nam plah, coconut milk and sometimes dried shrimp – but it is a 'dry' curry, ie simmered until the sauce is thick. It's as tasty cold as it is hot.

Tom Yum soup – A clear noodle broth which is very simple to make, and delicious. We're counting it as a Thai curry because it's hot and from Thailand, but in terms of experience it's closer to Japanese soups which are not so much cooked as assembled, with fresh vegetables, meat and fish and hot, savoury stock. It's often eaten as a starter, but can be a meal in itself.

Jungle curry – sounds like it might be a bit of a hectic experience, and indeed it is. It consists of a green or red curry base with extra things in which may include frog, if you're in the right (or wrong) part of Thailand. Most restaurant jungle curries will be amphibian-free, but they are usually hot, so be warned.

Either curry has gone to Mohammed Ali's head or he thinks he's taking spice to greater heights. In May 2006, the owner of the Sundarbon restaurant in Birmingham, enabled diners to get high – 2,000 feet up in the air to be precise – before coming back down to earth for a slap-up dinner. The *Birmingham Post* reported that the fly, wine and dine – or aerodinamix – experience was designed to make Sundarbon's customers feel a cut above the rest (in Birmingham there is serious competition between the thousands of curry houses that line its streets). Customers of the restaurant, said to include the likes of Girls Aloud and Westlife, would pay £80 to enjoy the ride. With increased carbon emissions not seeming to cause any lack of sleep for the man who likes to be called The Raj, the venture was deemed to be a success – although the in-flight snack and spice sounded as if they were in danger of ending up in someone's lap.

Perhaps he could take a leaf out of Salik Miah's book: serve your curry up with wings (in 2003, the BBC reported that Miah was a recycled Boeing 747 into a luxury Indian restaurant venue), but keep your plane, your feet and your curry on firm ground (apparently he intends to park it in a field in Potters Bar, although there is no sign of it yet).

CURRIED WORDS

On encountering the Portuguese version:

Now of the provision itself, for our large dishes, they were filled with rice dressed. And this rice was presented to us, some of it white, in its own proper colour, some of it yellow, with saffron, and some of it was made green, and some of it was put in purple colour... and with rice thus ordered, several of our dishes were furnished, and very many more of them with flesh of several kinds, and with hens and other sorts of fowl cut in pieces, as before observed in their Indian cookery. To these we had many jellie and culices; Rice ground to flour and then boyled and after sweetened with sugar, candy and rosewater to be eaten cold. The flower or rice mingled, with sweet almonds, made as small as they could, and with some of the most fleshy parts hens, stewed with it and after, the flesh beaten to pieces, that it could not be discerned all made sweet with rosewater and sugar candy, and scented with ambergreece which was another of our dishes and a most luscious one, which the Portugals call 'Manger Real', food for a King.

Rev Edward Terry, *Purchas and His Pilgrims*, 1625

*Alice and the White Rabbit took time out of their adventure
to work their way through Wonderland's curry guide.*

QUOTE UNQUOTE

*Ninety nine per cent of Indians do not have a tandoor and so
neither tandoori chicken nor naan are part of India's middle class
cuisine. This is even so in the Punjab, although some villages have
communal tandoors where rotis can be baked. Ninety five per cent
of Indians don't know what a vindaloo, jhal farezi or, for that
matter, a Madras curry is.*
Camellia Panjabi, Indian, author of 50 Great Curries of India (2000)

In 1912, Wilbur Scoville, an American chemist, devised a method to measure the hotness of chilli peppers. The Scoville Organoleptic Test involved blending pure ground chillis with a sugar and water solution, which was sipped by a panel of testers. The solutions were increasingly diluted until they no longer burned the mouth. A number was then assigned to that chilli pepper, based on how much it needed to be diluted before the tester could taste no heat.

Despite the Scoville testers' devotion to their task, the scale has been widely criticised, and alternative tests and scales have been devised, including the High-Performance Liquid Chromatography (HPLC) test, and the Gillett method. Nevertheless, the Scoville method has stood the test of time, and still offers a reliable guide – or perhaps a warning – to what you are about to receive. However, as individual types of pepper can vary from mild to hot, it can only ever be a guide.

0-100: includes most sweet peppers
500-1,000: includes New Mexican peppers
1,000-1,500: includes Espanola peppers
1,000-2,000: includes Ancho and Pasilla peppers
1,000-2,500: includes Cascabel and Cherry peppers
2,500-5,000: includes Jalapeño and Mirasol peppers
5,000-15,000: includes Serrano peppers
15,000-30,000: includes de Arbol peppers
30,000-50,000: includes Cayenne and Tabasco peppers
50,000-100,000: includes Chiltepin peppers
100,000-350,000: includes Scotch Bonnet and Thai peppers
200,000-300,000: includes Habanero peppers
16,000,000: the heat level of pure capsaicin, the substance that gives peppers their heat. The heat is created by capsaicin, which is found not in the seeds, but at the point where the seed is attached to the white membrane inside the pepper.

The hottest chilli pepper in the world is currently believed to be the Red Savina Habanero pepper, rated at 577,000 Scoville units. While chilli peppers may be edible, any food that comes with a warning (this one is from Larousse Gastronomique) should be treated with great respect: 'Try chillies and their products sparingly at first until acquainted with their flavour. The seeds inside a chilli are extremely hot and should be removed unless a fiery result is required. Capsaicin… is a severe irritant which can burn the skin, particularly delicate areas around the eyes and nails or any cuts. Always wash your hands thoroughly after preparing chillies and avoid touching your eyes; alternatively use disposable plastic gloves to prepare chillies.'

Number of people who were seriously ill after Japanese curry was 63
supposedly poisoned at a village festival in Japan in 1998

The capital's very first curry houses
Veeraswamy's Indian Restaurant, 99 Regent Street, London W1

Veeraswamy's Indian Restaurant was opened in 1927 by one Edward Palmer – the great grandson of an English general and Indian princess and manager of the Mughal Palace at the Empire Exhibition a few years earlier. Applauded by fashionable flapper pundits of the time, the traditional atmosphere led to the restaurants dubbing as 'The ex-Indian higher serviceman's curry club' – 'higher' being the operative word. Staff were brought over from India to help create a range of authentic dishes and many of those who were to form the backbone of the new curry restaurant learnt their trade there.

It was eventually sold to Sir William Steward MP, who ran it for 40 years and was labelled 'The curry king' by *The Times* (pre-Pat Chapman of course). Refurbished in 1996, the legend now operates simply as Veeraswamy, and dining under the management of owners Ranjit Mathrani, Namita Panjabi and Camellia Panjabi, and head chef Gopal Kochak is a more modern affair. As testament to its standing and success, Pandit Nehru, Indira Gandhi, Edward Prince of Wales, King Gustav of Sweden, King Hussein of Jordan, Charlie Chaplin and Marlon Brando have all illustrated their love of curry there.

BURNING QUESTIONS

What is a traditional Indian oven called?
Answer on page 151.

A CAPTIVE CURRY

Many famous figures have been gripped by curry. Nelson Mandela, for one, was so partial to 'an Indian' at the legendary Kapitan's in Johannesburg's inner city, he dreamt about the dish during his 27-year incarceration. As a young lawyer in the 1950s, he would pay the restaurant a daily visit to fuel up on his favourite meal made by life-long proprietor Majandit Ranshod. When Mandela heard that the restaurant might close before he was due to be released, he wrote to Ranshod to express his disappointment. With the chef cracking on for 80 years, and his retirement looming, it was a tough call – but Mandela's campaigning technique seemed to work. Kapitan's is still open, albeit for lunches only. While times have changed, the décor and the 'curry only' policy haven't. Along with Ranshod, much of the furniture has been there since the 1930s. Now, if Mandela wants to pull up his old pew, he can relax knowing it is still safely there.

CURRIED WORDS

On encountering Indian cookery:

They feed not freely on full dishes of mutton and beef as we, but much on rice boiled with pieces of flesh or dressed many other ways. They have not many roast or baked meats, but stew most of their flesh. Among many dishes of this kind, I will take notice of one they call deu pario [do-pyaza] made of venison cut in slices, to which they put onions and herbs, some roots with a little spice and butter: the most savoury meat I have ever tasted and do almost think it that very dish which Jacob made ready for his father, when he got the blessing.

Rev Edward Terry, *Purchas and His Pilgrims*, 1625

HOW THE CURRY HOUSE GOT ITS NAME

The 'Star of India'
*In the words of that literary Raj, Rudyard Kipling,
some things are 'just so'...*

The Star of India is a three-pronged accolade that has inspired restaurants from London's Old Brompton Road to San Diego.

For most, the local Star is most likely to relate to the 563.35-carat, golf ball-sized star sapphire that currently resides in the American Museum of Natural History, New York. The flawless gem was famously stolen in October 1964. Cat burglars – including one-time surfing champion Jack Murphy – climbed through a bathroom window finding the alarm was already dead. Sri Lanka's most wanted rock was eventually recovered from a Miami bus station. However, the Eagle Diamond – lifted at the same time – has never been seen again.

Over in San Diego, the restored *Star of India* is touted as the world's oldest seafaring ship. Built in 1863 in the Isle of Man, it originally launched as the *Eurterpe*, after the Greek goddess of music. It wasn't all plain sailing though: the ship came face to face with a cyclone in the Bay of Bengal and her first captain died on board. Her name was changed to the *Star of India* in 1906 and after 60 years dedicated service as a cargo ship to India, a passenger vessel hauling emigrants to New Zealand and a commercial salmon fishing facility, she finally retired in 1923.

The least-known Star story is that of the Most Exalted Order of the Star of India – founded by Queen Victoria in 1861 to honour Indian princes and chiefs, as well as British officers who served in India. Thankfully you don't need to have a knighthood to dine at your Star.

Number of new Wagamama restaurants opened around the world in the 65 last 14 years serving authentic Japanese curries and noodles

KOSHER CURRY

It was good news for the UK's curry-loving kosher Jews this year with curry companion Cobra getting the all clear. 'Kosher' refers to a dietary practice that specifies what can and cannot be eaten in reference to texts in the Bible – common non-kosher or impure foods often used in curries include pork, fish, prawns, yoghurt and some mixed spices. Causing something of a celebration for the staff at www.somethingjewish.co.uk, the drink was given the thumbs up by London Beth Din, which means even the Chief Rabbi can have one with his chicken tikka masala (as long as it's kosher, of course). The site was also pleased to welcome the city's first kosher Indian restaurant, Kavanna, opened in June 2006 – as, it seems by other reports, were its keen north-west London clientele. A range of kosher simtom Indian curry paste, poppadums and pickles are apparently also on sale in Barnet supermarkets for the first time – Hendon and Golders Green have a 1,000-strong Indian Jewish community so it's welcome relief for them. Thanks to one Nathan Moses, they have already been tucking into samosas, bhajis, pilau rice, vegetable korma and dahl from a local Hendon bakery. The rest of the UK's kosher Jews eagerly await...

MEATLOAF GETS IT

After Meatloaf and Tim Curry co-starred in 1975's *The Rocky Horror Picture Show*, meatloaf and curry joined forces once again to produce another 1970s hit... curried meatloaf.

2lb ground lean lamb or meatloaf mixture
1 teaspoon grated fresh ginger, or $\frac{1}{2}$ teaspoon ground ginger
3 cloves garlic, crushed
1 onion, grated
2 teaspoons ground coriander
$\frac{1}{4}$ teaspoon paprika
$\frac{1}{8}$ teaspoon ground cloves
$\frac{1}{8}$ teaspoon ground cinnamon
1 teaspoon salt
1 egg, beaten
1 tub curry sauce

Combine the ground meat with the rest of the ingredients. Mix thoroughly. Pack in to a pan loaf, cover tightly with aluminium foil, and bake in a moderate oven for about one hour. Turn the meatloaf out onto a serving dish, reserving any juices, and keep warm. Pour over curry sauce.

Hard work, more hard work and marketing.
Tommy Miah, owner of Edinburgh's Raj restaurant, on his recipe
for curry-house success, quoted on DesPardes.com, the specialist
news site for Indian expatriates, 2003

BURNING QUESTIONS

Which Indian dish literally means 'twice the onions'?
Answer on page 151.

JOIN THE CLUB

*Who can lay claim to the title of 'founder of the original Curry
Club'? Rupees at the ready, place your bets here...*

The Curry Club was established in 1962, the first president being Vic Gardener, 'to form a friendly bond between members at meetings to be held at regular intervals for the purpose of enjoying a good Indian curry luncheon'. Many of the initial 'members' were employed on the Barbican project – work started on London's landmark residential, commercial and arts complex in the year of the club's inauguration. The ethos of the group was that of a gentlemen's dining club, managed by a committee elected from the membership – a very Raj affair. Meetings are still held at the India Club in the Strand Continental Hotel, London, on the last Friday of alternate months, from January. Conduct reeks of the Raj, with members expected to observe the strict dress code of jacket and club tie. Formal addresses are then made by the president and other invited speakers, followed by a loyal toast. Central to the proceedings, however, is the food with bar nibbles, and then a comprehensive set lunch: 'Anglo-Indian in nature with a Southern Indian bias – well-spiced, but not excessively hot – and is rather more authentic than available at most high street restaurants.' A typical menu includes: a starter of poppadums, mango chutney, Indian salad and a mysterious 'chef's special'; this is followed by meat curry, chicken or seafood curry, two vegetable dishes, rice and breads; the finale is fruit, ice-cream and an ambiguous 'Indian speciality'. Gentlemen who feel they have the necessary nuance to meet all the credentials – and brave the adventurous menu – can register their vote for Gardener's Curry Club at www.thecurryclub.co.uk.

Most of us already know how to cook rice; although, it's not always as easy as it sounds. The secret is to rinse before use and to leave it to simmer without upsetting the grain. But that's not the only consideration to factor in when preparing a curry...

Short, medium or long?

Long grain rice is the traditional accompaniment to curry (unless you're eating Thai curry, in which case sticky rice or jasmine rice will do much better). It's drier than its short-grain equivalent, and it's also lighter and easier to digest (short grain rice is much more dense). Long grain rice is also used to make pilaf and paella, and is a favourite for English housewives in rice pudding dishes.

White or brown?

Brown rice is simply white rice that has not had the bran covering the rice grains removed, so it comes in exactly the same form (long, short and medium), but needs more water and takes longer to cook. As brown rice still has the bran in place, it's a much better source of fibre.

Think organic

Rice is said to grow better when it is produced in good soil, as the minerals and nutrients it contains are passed on to the rice. The same could be said for the pesticides and chemical fertilisers used on non-organic soil. If you do use non-organic rice, make sure you wash the rice before use and skim any foam that appears when you are boiling the rice. Some nutritionists believe that it contains starch and toxins.

What about wild rice?

It's delicious, but it's not actually rice. In fact, it's a seed grain from a grass that isn't actually in the rice family. But that's not to say that you can't eat it with your curry. It's a perfect accompaniment to spicy vegetable dishes.

CURRIED WORDS

'Cooks with peire newe conceytes,
choppynge, stampynge and gryndynge.
Many new curies alle day pey ar contryvynge and
fyndynge þat provotethe þe peple to perelles of passage
prouz peyne soore pyndynge and prouz nice excesse of
such receytes of þe life to make a endynge.'

FJ Furnell in *Manners and Meals in Olden Times* (1868), repeating a passage from a fifteenth-century treatise against nouvelle cuisine.

68 *Date in twentieth century that Doris Ady published* Curries from the Sultan's Kitchen, *in Australia*

Ron the Giant tucks into his favourite dish, curried humans.

FLY ME TO THE GAME

A report by the BBC on 13 June 2006, highlighted just how curry crazy the UK nation had become, when a group of football-mad musicians watching the World Cup while in Germany ordered a celebration curry to be flown in from a Somerset restaurant. The celebration in question: not the 'golden balls' of the England team (eventually kicked out in the quarters by the hot footwork of the Portuguese team and some very fine pickling of their own). In fact, the feast was ordered as a reward for getting the band's latest single into the dance charts. The aptly named Opposite World (well 1,287 kilometres across the continent at least) ordered ramo dakhna chicken, mirchi fish, lamb karahi and Bombay king prawns, together with a selection of rice, naan breads and starters from Bombay Rice in Bath. It cost £1,600 in total, and was carried out by equally jubilant restaurant manager, Abdul Nasir.

In 1999, British health officials warned that curry chefs may be causing asthma and allergies with the use of excessive good colourings. Perhaps urged on by tikka and tandoori fans who thought the correct colour of their food should be sunset pink, as opposed to spiced and oven-baked brown, more and more restaurants had been falling back on artificial colourings to make their curries more appealing. A trading standards swoop on restaurants in the West Midlands' Balti Belt found more than half of the most colourful dishes contained levels of additives that would breach safety rules under some circumstances. Some dishes contained colouring levels up to 16 times that permitted by law in a sauce. The most concern was awarded to dishes containing the colourings Tartrazine, Sunset Yellow and Ponceau 4R, the repeated overexposure of which is thought to lead to oversensitivity to allergies. Although council officials and health experts petitioned for changes in the law (colouring legislation only applies to sauces, not meat or rice), a similar report in 2005 showed that curry houses in South Yorkshire were still producing much of the same. As one owner of a colour-free chain of curry houses stressed, public awareness needs to be changed to sway the chefs – the redder the curry doth not make it more tasty or hot. Unless it's made with copious amounts of red chillis of course!

FLOCK-PAPER FAVOURITES: JALFREZI

Deciphering the curry house menu...

A very British dish, jalfrezi or jhal frezi was thought to have originated at the time of the Raj when Anglo-Indian housekeepers were instructed to curry cold meat with onions and chilli – something Mrs Beeton also prescribed in her 1861 *Book of Household Management*. It includes recipes for no less than 14 curries, often cited as 'suitable for cold meats'. Jalfrezi literally means 'hot fry' or 'dry fry', but the term may be better translated to local UK lingo as 'stir fry', where leftovers from the very British roast – chicken, lamb or beef and perhaps some potatoes – would be cooked up in a pan and served up waste-not-want-not style. The jalfrezi we see on our menus does stick to the stir-fry method, but the ingredients of this relatively dry dish tend to include visible and crunchy green peppers, onions, tomatoes and an abundance of green chillis, which can make it hot on the heels of the vindaloo and phall. Hopefully the marinated meat used in curry houses today is as fresh and piquant as the taste the other ingredients impart...

Heat factor: Hot to trot.

RANALD MARTIN'S CURRY POWDER

A favourite blend, from *Curry Recipes: Selected from the Unpublished Collection of Sir Ranald Martin* by Mrs Jessop Hulton, 1938. Medium hot.

1lb best powdered tumeric
³/₄lb powdered coriander seed
3oz powdered ginger
2oz black powdered pepper
1¹/₂oz cayenne powdered pepper
1¹/₂oz powdered cardamom seed
¹/₂oz powdered caraway seed
80 finely powdered cloves

The whole mixture to be well mixed and put into a stoppered dry bottle or glass jar. Two tablespoonfuls will be enough to curry a fowl.

SPICE GUYS

*A key player in the Spice Trail, Vasco Da Gama
opened the world's first all-water trade route*

1498:

On [22 May] these same boats came again alongside, when the captain-major sent one of the convicts to Calicut, and those with whom he went took him to two Moors from Tunis, who could speak Castilian and Genoese. The first greeting that he received was in these words: 'May the Devil take thee! What brought you hither?' They asked what he sought so far away from home, and he told them that we came in search of Christians and of spices. They said: 'Why does not the King of Castile, the King of France, or the Signoria of Venice send thither?' He said that the King of Portugal would not consent to their doing so, and they said he did the right thing. After this conversation they took him to their lodgings and gave him wheaten bread and honey. When he had eaten he returned to the ships, accompanied by one of the Moors, who was no sooner on board, than he said these words: 'A lucky venture, a lucky venture! Plenty of rubies, plenty of emeralds! You owe great thanks to God, for having brought you to a country holding such riches!' We were greatly astonished to hear his talk, for we never expected to hear our language spoken so far away from Portugal.

Vasco Da Gama, *Round Africa to India*, c. 1497-1498

Chicken, beef, lamb, fish or even goat – but surely crocodile curry is taking things a bit far? 'Exotic' food company Edible certainly don't think so, with green crocodile curry working its way onto the menu in 2004, for a small fee of £10.95. A Thai-style, green concoction (suitable camouflage for the croc in question), the tinned dish is apparently made with 'tender morsels of farm-raised crocodile fillet and rare Thai vegetables'. The dish is also aimed at health-conscious curry fans, with the delicate white meat 'low in cholesterol'.

Apparently Siamese crocodiles are 'farmed in Thailand under strict accordance with convention in trade in endangered species protocol (CITES) and imported under strict EU and UK regulations.' However, this species became rare in the wild due to illegal harvesting of its skin and meat. Even with a dramatic comeback thanks to captive propagation, there's more than a touch of irony – particularly for the poor croc who has only just started to thrive again. Left to its own devices, it could live to a ripe old age. Although death by Thai curry could be favoured by some, it's not advisable to get up close and ask a Siamese croc what he thinks about this one.

GLOBAL WARMING: AMERICA

On the spice trail and around the world on the good ship Curry...

In Lizzie Collingham's *Curry: A Tale of Cooks and Conquerors* (2006), the first chicken curry 'probably first appeared on an American restaurant menu at either the el ranchero in Yuba City or at Pancho's in Selma' in the 1920s. In the late 1890s, a small number of Punjabi men began to arrive on the west coast of America, to try and make their fortunes as farm hands before travelling home. They brought Indian 'curry' cuisine with them, but new laws soon prevented them from bringing their wives and families over, too. This led to a wave of Mexican-Indian marriages, and the combination of spices resulted in a kind of Mexican-Hindu cuisine – with the jalapeno pepper as the main source of heat. Over on the East coast, Indian ship-jumpers made their way to New York, although a 1923 US Supreme Court ruling hailing Indians as aliens 'ineligible for American citizenship' initially prevented them from settling down. The influx of Indian workers brought over later in the twentieth century, to staff call centres and lend their hi-tech expertise, ensured curry was safely on the American menu alongside Kentucky Fried Chicken and that ubiquitous national dish, the Big Mac.

MRS BEETON'S CURRY WISDOM

Lobster Curry (an Entrée)

Ingredients: 1 lobster, 2 onions, 1oz butter, 1 tablespoonful of curry-powder, $^1/_2$ pint of medium stock, No 105, the juice of $^1/_2$ a lemon.

Mode – Pick the meat from the shell, and cut it into nice square pieces; fry the onions of a pale brown in the butter, stir in the curry-powder and stock, and simmer till it thickens, when put in the lobster; stew the whole slowly for $^1/_2$ hour, and stir occasionally; and just before sending to table, put in the lemon-juice. Serve boiled rice with it, the same as for other curries.

Time – altogether, $^3/_4$ hour.

Average cost – 3s.

Seasonable – at any time.

Isabella Beeton – aka 'Mrs Beeton',
Book of Household Management, 1861

QUOTE UNQUOTE

I have known Noon (no-one knows him as anything else) for 10 years and it's thanks to him that I once – for the only time in my life – cheated on my dinner guests. Hidden in the kitchen were a variety of packs of his wonderful, factory-made curries.
Delia Smith, British cookery writer, on her friend,
ready-meals tycoon Sir Gulam Noon

THE CONVICT CURRYMAKER

Readers of *The Guardian*'s society pages may recognise the name Erwin James from a regular column written by him, for the paper, while serving a life sentence in jail. The column detailed his experiences of prison life to help shed some inside light on part of the UK's crime and punishment system. James was released after 20 years, in 2004, but he continued to have his say and has published several books. In December 2005, he reminisced about learning to make curry from another inmate, Mr Patel, also serving life. While Mr Patel died behind bars, his tins of spice and his curry secrets, learnt over some weeks lived on through eager chef James. Even pilchard curry – when cooked under Mr Patel's proud supervision of course – tasted good on the inside (as opposed to the usual prison fare perhaps), although James suggests some 'strange ways' of serving it on top of pasta with a sprinkling of cheese and some chapattis.

Books commonly say that Indians do not use curry powder. This may have been true in the days when even the servants had servants and the masala of fresh ginger, garlic, onion, coconut, green chile, and spices was ground on the stone freshly for each dish. But today, a First World cost of servants has caught up with Third World households, and ready-ground spice mixtures are no longer beyond the pale.

Tom Stobart, author of *The Cook's Encyclopedia*, writing in 1980

HOW THE CURRY HOUSE GOT ITS NAME

The 'Shalamar'
In the words of that literary Raj, Rudyard Kipling, some things are 'just so'…

The 1970s saw a rush of all things Shalamar. With an all-singing all-dancing pop group – they of lyrca leggings, 'A Night to Remember' and 'Don't Get Stopped in Beverley Hills' fame – plus numerous curry houses all operating under the same name, by the 1980s the Shalamar or Shalimar epic was to have become something of an epidemic. Indeed TV's *Soul Train* host Don Cornelius and the show's A&R man Dick Griffey were responsible for launching the Motown medley 'Uptown Festival' on the world in 1977. However, it was Punjabi restaurateur Asif Khan who first brought the name to UK fame with his pre-war curry house in Soho's Wardour Street. A variation on spelling, the Shalimar, referenced another of Mughal Emperor Shajahan's labours of love, the Shalimar Gardens of Lahore. Laid out in three descending terraces – the Bestower of Pleasure, the Bestower of Goodness and the Bestower of Life – the gardens were irrigated by a specially built canal that ran a lengthy 161 kilometres from Rajpot (now Madhpur) and discharged into a marble basin centrepiece in Shalimar. The canal also fed 410 fountains and five water cascades that still provide welcome relief to sun-parched visitors today. Within the gardens are pavilions, minarets, resting places, sleeping chambers, a hammam or royal bath, and even a dream place for his favourite wife. The Shalimar is now a hit curry house in San Francisco, New York, Liverpool and Budapest. It is the name of a beach resort in Florida and was launched as a scent of the exotic in 1920s Paris. You can live in it, wear it and eat in it – just remember those romantic roots when you take your next bite of bhuna.

FOUND IN TRANSLATION

Some help reading old Indian recipes, should someone deem fit to pass a secret curry sauce down...

Hindustani	English
1 Seer	2lb
1 Chittack	2oz
1 Tolah	$^{3}/_{4}$oz
Adruk	green ginger
Chenee	brown sugar
Dalchenee	cinnamon
Degchee	cooking vessel
Dhunnia	coriander seeds
Etatchee	cardamoms
Gol Mirich, or Meerich	black pepper
Goor	molasses sugar
Gram (chuna)	split peas
Huldee, or Huldi	turmeric
Jeera	cumin seeds
Kismis	raisins
Kutch-Kutch	poppy seed
Lall Mirich, or Meerich	red chillis, dry chillis and red pepper
Long	cloves
Lusoon, or Lussoon	garlic

TIKKAS IN A TWIST

While curry sometimes gets a rep for giving people something of a wind problem, on 28 July 2005, Birmingham's famous 'balti triangle' was reeling from a wind problem of its own. In fact a freak summer tornado, with wind speeds of up to 135mph, shook the area causing extensive damage to buildings, gardens and vehicles. Nineteen people were also injured. More reminiscent of *The Wizard of Oz* than a July day in the Midlands, roofs were seen flying through the air and trees fell at whim in the worst hit areas. Birmingham's balti industry was left reeling and especially badly affected were those businesses in the popular balti belt of Ladypool Road. A real jewel in the crown for the city – not only for local customers, but also as a real tourist attraction – thankfully by 2006, repairs were nearly done. Birmingham's baltis can once again be enjoyed without the risk of the roof falling in. Restaurants only request that customers keep their own wind under control while inside.

Number in thousands of crocuses needed to produce five pounds of stigmas, which after being toasted, yield merely one pound of saffron 75

*Even at the dawn of the curry age, lager reserves
were severely depleted.*

AMONG THE VILLAGE FOLK

Numbers of the men go down to the river or to the village tank to
bathe, while the women sprinkle the front and back yards of their
dwellings with cow dung. This is done to drive away the goddess of
ill luck, who will not come to a place where the cow, a sacred animal
in the eyes of all Hindus, is present. Next the women sweep out their
houses, milk the cows and goats, clean their cooking vessels, and
make ready the first meal. To this the men return at about eight
o'clock, and sit down on the ground to eat rice or chuppaties. The
latter are flat, round, unleavened cakes of meal, and form the daily
bread of both rich and poor. With these foods they use various sauces
and condiments, pickles and curries, and drink buttermilk. When the
men have finished eating, the women take what is left in the dishes.
The food is eaten from brass plates or plantain leaves, and raised to
the mouth with the hands.

The men now go back to their labour in the fields or their
workshops, and the women fetch water, collect fuel, weave, pound
rice or grain, grind spices for curry powder, and get the midday meal
ready and serve it at noon...

John Finnemore, *Home Life in India*, 1912

Don't forget to order the chutney..

Danish..*chutney*
Dutch..*Indiase zoetzure saus*
French........................... *condiment (à la/au* insert fruit name here)
German..*chutney*
Italian..*salsa*
Portuguese...*molho picante*
Spanish...*salsa picante*
Swedish...*slags indisk pickles*

CURRIES FROM THE REST OF ASIA

Thailand, Malaysia, Japan and Indonesia all have their own forms of curry, with many subtle variations

Thailand
Meat, fish or vegetables served in a sauce spiced up with chilli peppers and sweetened with Kaffir lime leaves and coconut milk. Dishes are generally described by colour: red (from the red chilli), green (from the green chilli) and yellow (from the use of turmeric and cumin).

Malaysia
Similar to Thai curries in the use of coconut milk, chilli and turmeric, curries in Malaysia can include anything from fish heads to eggs and goat.

China
Chunky portions of meat, fish and vegetables typically served in a mildly spicy yellow curry sauce, with plenty of rice on the side. Chinese curry is also served, like much else in the country, with white pepper, soy sauce and hot chilli oil.

Japan
Known as 'kare raisu', the Japanese form of curry is one of the country's most popular dishes. Less hot than its Indian and Thai counterparts, it generally consists of beef served in a thick, almost sweet sauce, served on rice and accompanied by Japanese pickles. Unlike other forms of Japanese food, it is always eaten with a spoon.

Indonesia
Meat or chicken served in a thick brown coconut sauce.

BAPU'S BIRYANI

An ancient family recipe that never fails to get even the most wayward kids home to see the folks. Serves two adults and three grown children.

Leg lamb (cubed, fat removed)
4-5 cups basmati rice
1 onion (finely sliced)
1 green chilli (sliced)
lemon juice
1 tablespoon garam masala
1 tablespoon vegetable oil
saffron or turmeric

Marinade
200ml plain yoghurt
1 tablespoon garam masala
$1^{1}/_{2}$ tablespoon chilli/garlic/ginger paste

1) Marinade lamb for minimum 24 hours to tenderise
2) Partially cook basmati rice, drain and put aside
3) Brown onions
4) Heat oil in large pan for one minute. Layer from bottom up: meat, remaining marinade, rice and onions
5) Add chilli, lemon juice and sprinkle of saffron or turmeric with water
6) Seal pan tightly and cook on very low heat for $1^{1}/_{2}$ hours
7) Mix layers and serve with sliced onions, fresh coriander and a dollop of family pride

---

THE CROWN QUEEN OF CURRY

The majestically titled coronation chicken was invented by florist Constance Spry and chef Rosemary Hume, and served at the coronation lunch of Queen Elizabeth II in 1953. The recipe subsequently appeared in the *Constance Spry Cookery Book* of 1956, and was almost certainly inspired by jubilee chicken – a similar chicken, curry and mayo dish prepared for the silver jubilee of George V in 1935. Coronation chicken also included superior curry paste, onion, tomato purée, red wine, apricot halves, whipping cream, a bay leaf, juice from a lemon and watercress to garnish. Both dishes were designed to be served cold, perhaps so the public didn't have to labour over a hot stove on such an important occasion, or maybe because it was easier to serve as a cold main course at a large banquet. Fresh curry spice, almonds, raisins and crème fraîche are common ingredients today, and the unnervingly bright yellow dish can now be found in sarnies or tubs from Pret A Manger to Marks & Spencer.

SPICE GUYS

Steering along the coast of a new land in 1492

I desired to set out today for the island which I think must be Cipangu [Cuba], according to the signs these people make, indicative of its size and riches... It is better to go where there is great entertainment, so I say that it is not reasonable to wait, but rather to continue the voyage and inspect much land, until some very profitable country is reached, my belief being that it will be rich in spices. That I have no knowledge of the products causes me the greatest sorrow in the world, for I see a thousand kinds of trees, each one with its own special trait, as well as a thousand kinds of herbs with their flowers; yet I know none of them.

Christopher Columbus, from his personal journals

QUOTE UNQUOTE

Wagner, Beethoven and Hendrix might have chanced the vindaloo but Mozart, Debussy and John Denver were probably korma or, perhaps, dhansak guys on a daring night.
Ian Anderson, Scottish, frontman of Jethro Tull,
in his online curry guide

A ROYAL LAD IN THE HOUSE

Getting Prince Charles on side has been a stroke of marketing genius for Brick Lane favourite Aladin. Traditionally a meeting place for the large Bangladeshi community in the area (many immigrants from Sylhet settled there) the Aladin was popularised when Charlie spoke about it on LBC radio in the 1980s. The restaurant was keen to cash in on the royal recommendation and quickly tacked a picture of the prince to its window – albeit faded some 20 years or more on. The faded snap is still there and menus invite customers to ask staff to hear the transmission tape, even to this day. One source told a story of how the rumour of royal recognition has even spread across the pond to America. On visiting Brick Lane in the mid-1990s to visit a fledgling designer fashion house struggling to make ends meet in the then seedy Cheshire Street (now packed with trendy stores), the swanky Neiman Marcus buyers requested their lunch be delivered from there. The collection of clothes was snapped up, although the 'cute' curry could have had something to do with it. No one has been tempted to change the restaurant's name to the Bucks Palace – yet.

On the spice trail and around the world on the good ship Curry...

In 1786, Britain secured rule of Penang Island, off the Malay Peninsula. It became part of colonial India, and by 1909 the Empire had spread to include the whole of Malaya, now Malaysia, and Singapore. India already had links with Malaya, with Pallavas and Cholas – ancient Indian ruling dynasties – establishing trading posts there, well before the thirteenth century. But by the time the British arrived, their legacy had been more or less absorbed into an equally strong Malay culture, although Mughal staples such as kebabs were already morphing onto the menu. It was with the arrival of southern Indian Tamils – brought in as cheap labour in the mid-nineteenth century, and Indian traders from Sindh and Gujurat, that the Malay-Indian 'curry' really took off. Mamak food – or the food of the Malay Tamil Muslims (an off-shoot of then common Malay-Tamil inter-marriages) gives a Malay twist to Indian dishes: popular nasi goreng (fried rice) is an off-shoot of biryani, while the addition of coconut milk results in a classic Malay korma.

ELEPHANTS NEVER FORGET

While the above may not be true for Indian or African elephants, turmeric – a spicy ingredient used in curries originating from both continents – could help to preserve the human memory. Newspaper reports in 2001 cited a study from a team of researchers from the University of California, Los Angeles, who believe that turmeric could play a role in slowing down the progression of neurodegenerative disease. This could explain why rates of Alzheimer's disease – a progressive brain disorder that gradually destroys the memory and is the most common cause of dementia – are much lower among the elderly in India, than in their Western peers. According to previous studies,

Alzheimer's affects just 1% of people over the age of 65, living in some Indian villages; among UK citizens of the same age group, the Alzheimer's Society describes dementia as affecting one person in 20 – more than five times more. The society's director of research, Dr Richard Harvey, maintained that the active ingredient curcumin had both antioxidant and anti-inflammatory properties, which when reproduced in drugs, could potentially be used to help prevent the disease. Researchers also found that turmeric could aid digestion, help fight infection and guard against heart attacks. Whoever said curry wasn't good for you? Now where did I put that takeaway menu?

Year in the eighteenth century in which the first commercial curry powder appeared

QUOTE UNQUOTE

*By activating several areas of the tongue simultaneously,
we are literally dazzling our taste buds to a state of confusion.
Traditional British foods fail to do this, due to the basic flavour
combinations. When we crave a curry it seems our taste buds
are literally crying out for stimulation.*
Professor Stephen Gray, from Nottingham Trent University,
explaining the effects of curry to the BBC on 25 October 2000

BURNING QUESTIONS

What would you get if you ordered a 'Bombay Duck'?
Answer on page 151.

MRS BEETON'S CURRY WISDOM

Mullagatawny Soup

Ingredients: 2 tablespoonfuls of curry powder, 6 onions, 1 clove of
garlic, 1oz of pounded almonds, a little lemon-pickle, or mango-juice,
to taste; 1 fowl or rabbit, 4 slices of lean bacon; 2 quarts of medium
stock, or, if wanted very good, best stock.

Mode: Slice and fry the onions of a nice colour; line the stewpan with
the bacon; cut up the rabbit or fowl into small joints, and slightly
brown them; put in the fried onions, the garlic, and stock, and simmer
gently till the meat is tender; skim very carefully, and when the meat
is done, rub the curry powder to a smooth batter; add it to the soup
with the almonds, which must be first pounded with a little of the
stock. Put in seasoning and lemon-pickle or mango-juice to taste, and
serve boiled rice with it.

Time – 2 hours.

Average cost – 1s. 6d. per quart, with stock No. 105.

Seasonable – in winter.

Sufficient for – 8 persons.

Note: This soup can also be made with breast of veal, or calf's head.
Vegetable mullagatawny is made with veal stock, by boiling and
pulping chopped vegetable marrow, cucumbers, onions, and
tomatoes, and seasoning with curry powder and cayenne. Nice pieces
of meat, good curry powder, and strong stock, are necessary to make
this soup good.

Isabella Beeton – aka 'Mrs Beeton',
***Book of Household Management*, 1861**

CURRIED WORDS

Dispelling the myth that all Indians ate rice

It is a popular impression that the poor of India live almost exclusively upon rice, which is very cheap and nourishing, hence it is possible for a family to subsist upon a few cents a day. This is one of the many delusions that are destroyed when you visit the country. Rice in India is a luxury that can be afforded only by the people of good incomes, and throughout four-fifths of the country is sold at prices beyond the reach of common working people. Sixty per cent of the population live upon wheat, barley, fruit, various kinds of pulses and maize. Rice can be grown only in hot and damp climates, where there are ample means of irrigation, and only where the conditions of soil, climate and water supply allow its abundant production does it enter into the diet of the working classes. Three-fourths of the people are vegetarians, and live upon what they produce themselves.

William Eleroy Curtis, *Modern India*, 1905

A CURRY FOR CANCER

More medical medals for curry, this time celebrating its potential in helping to combat cancer. That doesn't mean you should head down the local curry house now and order mountains of korma – in fact, creamy dishes like this made with lots of meat and often colour additives can cause more harm than good. The key is in the curcumin, found in turmeric (one of the spices and the main colour in curry powder). In 2000, researchers at the oncology department of Leicester University noticed that out of 500 patients diagnosed with colon cancer, only two were Asian – this, in a city where 20% of the city's population are of Asian origin.

Tests are still underway, but research in the US has already suggested that spice could block or shrink tumours. In the mean time Cancer Research Campaign director Professor Gordon McVie praised curries for their high fruit and vegetable content and the fibre contained in its most popular side dish, rice. This doesn't usually apply to the typical curries we eat in restaurants, however, counteracted Luci Daniels, vice chair of the British Dietetic Association. So, if you want to reap the benefits of curry while you wait, the best advice is to do as the Indian's do and cook up your own with plenty of veggies, pulses and curcumin-rich spice.

The essence of a Thai curry – and we're counting pretty much everything vaguely hot and savoury in the Thai culinary repertoire here – is chilli, galangal and that fish sauce stuff. This... condiment, seasoning, whatever you want to call it, is one of the most bizarre foodstuffs known to mankind, and hence deserves a whole section simply for contemplation of its strangeness. There are some foods which make you pause and think, well, who decided that was edible? Blowfish, bird's nest soup (made from swallows' saliva, don't you know?), wheat, things like that. And in that category is fish sauce, or nam plah. Who was it who worked out in the first place that liquified fish – for yes, this is what you are consuming in your beef rendang – would be nice when mixed up with other foods?

One might theorise that its origins were similar to those of Worcestershire sauce, which was discovered by accident when its manufacturers unwittingly left a barrel of tamarind sauce sitting in the cellar for a year. One might well theorise that, and one would be half right. Nam plah is Thai for 'fish water' and it is made from small fish such as anchovies by a gradual process of liquefaction (in the sun), fermentation and filtration. Unlike Mr Lea and Mr Perrins' discovery, though, it's no accident, at least in human memory: some form has been made since ancient times in Asia and even, it seems, by the Romans. But while fish sauce in one sense testifies to the things that don't change in life, its current provenance reflects the things that, unfortunately, do. While it used to be made in south-east Asia from fish caught both in fresh and saltwater, pollution and dams in the freshwater sources of the region have largely killed off the former process.

Still, hooray for nam plah! On its own, it's unspeakable (or at least, smells it); in a curry, it's heavenly. You can even use it in non-Thai dishes such as meat marinades and milkshakes (OK, made up the last one). A yet more bizarre foodstuff along similar lines is the Swedish *lutefisk*, which is cod covered in the stuff they make soap from and buried until it jellifies. The difference being that while no Thai curry is complete without a dash of nam plah, even the Swedes won't touch *lutefisk*.

QUOTE UNQUOTE

Many of the original pioneers of our glorious past passed away without the recognition they deserved. We don't want this to happen in the future.
Enam Ali, editor of *Spice*, on why he created the British Curry Awards

Tamarind

The curved brown pea pod of the tamarind tree is thought to originate in eastern Africa, although it now grows extensively throughout southern Asia, the West Indies and the Indian subcontinent where is also known as the 'date of India'. A useful souring agent in the absence of vinegar (the Portuguese famously used it to create the classic vindaloo), it is widely used in Gujarat and southern India in a range of lentil dishes, chutneys and of course, curries. Although some recipes use the pod, the most classic form of tamarind is as a paste or concentrate made by pressing the shiny black seeds into a fibrous mass. With pectin as one of its main components, tamarind both stores well and is a main ingredient in a variety of pickles, jams and sauces – without tamarind there would no Lea & Perrins iconic Worcestershire Sauce! In the Hindu religion, tamarind has acquired similarly holy status, in association with the wedding of the god Krishna, celebrated each November. However, tamarind also has its dark side: Victorian Brits in Goa, nicknamed Lugimlees or 'tamarind heads' supposedly wore a pod of tamarind in their ears to stop the locals from harassing them – apparently the pods were inhabited by demons, too. As the throat-scorching vindaloo also proves, the humble tamarind may not be such an innocent ingredient after all…

GOING JAPANESE

Hot on the heels of the Ramen Museum, the Yokohama Curry Museum arrived in January 2001 to help represent Japan's obsession with food, and in particular, curry. Visitors are whisked away by sari-wearing staff and the place is adorned with kitschy Indian motifs (signals of the dish's roots). Housed in a re-creation of a late nineteenth-century Yokohama port, the place also guides interested parties through the history of the area – here it becomes clear that Yokohama was one of the first ports of call for Western foods such as milk, bread and ice-cream; curry was also said to have first been eaten here in 1863, by Indians on a boat. With a barrage of special effects and interactive exhibits visitors may well work up an appetite at the museum. Luckily, there are no less than seven restaurants on board: three Indian, one serving Indian and 'European curry', one Thai and two Japanese. Unfortunately the highlights to be found at www.currymuseum.com will be lost in translation to all those who cannot read Japanese.

Princess Sibpan Sonakul's recipe for Thai curry paste from *The International Wine and Food Society's Guide to Far Eastern Cookery*, Robin Howe, 1969.

7-10 dried chillis, split and seeded
1 teaspoon salt
1 teaspoon peppercorns
2 teaspoon cumin seeds
2 teaspoons fresh coriander, chopped
1/2 teaspoon lemon or lime peel, grated
2 tablespoons lemongrass, finely chopped
1 tablespoon finely shredded kha (soapnut)
1 tablespoon garlic
1 tablespoon shallot
1 teaspoon salted shrimp paste or soy sauce

1) Soak chillis in water and pound to paste with salt
2) Work down list adding remaining ingredients
3) Pound each into paste until fine
4) Use paste for special Thai curry of choice

BEND IT LIKE BECKHAM

'Anyone can cook aloo gobi, but who can bend a ball like Beckham?' Such was the key line from Gurinder Chadha's 2002 hit movie *Bend It Like Beckham*. It tells the story of one Indian girl's struggle – Jess, played by Parminder Nagra, now of *ER* fame – to make her way in the modern world. Her family has other plans, including teaching her to cook a complete Indian dinner, marry a nice Indian boy and go to university. Meanwhile, her best friend's mum is only making things worse by accusing the football-mad pair of being lesbians and trying to disprove any racist tendencies to Jess with comments like: 'You know I cooked a lovely curry last night.' The director of *Bhaji on the Beach* (1993) and *What's Cooking?* (2000) filmed most of the film's scenes in London's curry capital of Southall – providing some authentic fodder for the cast and crew.

Apparently Beckham himself doesn't say no to a curry. After qualifying England for the World Cup in 2002, *The Observer Food Monthly* reported him as celebrating with 'his favourite' chicken korma in Manchester curry house Shimla Pinks. It failed to say whether he was any good with a gobi.

According to Pat Chapman on his website www.patchapman.co.uk, possible contenders for the origin of the word curry include:

Karhi, Kadhi or Kudhi – Gujarati soup-like, sour and slightly sweet dish, with its various spellings has been a Gujarati favourite for nearly 1,000 years. We know that, because a recipe for yoghurt beaten with gram flour, made golden with turmeric and asafoetida appears in early writings. This dish would have been eaten by the first English traders to arrive in India in 1608.

Kari, Kuri or Turkuri – 'Kari' in Tamil means 'pepper', and writings from c. 300AD tell that meat cooked with pepper was called Thallikari or just Kari. Later this evolved into a spicy stew with turmeric, coconut, black urid lentils, dry red chillis, which is found in southern India to this day under the same name, Kari or Kuri or Turkuri. This is the derivation given in *The Oxford Dictionary*.

Karahi or Karai or Kadahi, etc – The ubiquitous wok-like cooking pot used all over India. Quite a strong case as the derivation, but no proof.

Kari phulia or Kurri patta or Kari phulia. Bursunga (Bengali) or Curry – A soft, pale green, leaf (growing up to 4cm in length) used for flavouring. Despite its name, the leaf has a lemony fragrance, and no hint of curry.

Karil – Goan Canarese word meaning spicy food; referred to in writings as early as 1512 and 1563 and remains as the Portuguese word for curry. Not likely to be the derivation.

Koresh – An aromatic Iranian stew, whose roots go back to the days of the great Persian empire, which was at its height over 2,500 years ago.

Korma, Koorma, Kurma – In India, 'korma' refers to a slow cooking style, where only ghee or oil (and no water) is used in the initial cooking. The early English ambassadors to India occasionally ate at the Moghul courts, and would have certainly eaten this dish. A coincidence of alliteration, but not a derivation.

Lekkerie – The Dutch, who were in India by the late seventeenth century have their own derivation. They say it was used in their Indonesian curries, and that it derived from the word 'Lekker' meaning 'delicious'. A coincidence, ruled out by the timings of Dutch arrival.

Curing – An ancient process whereby meat and fish are dried by smoking or salting. Given that few English recipes used spices, right up to the last few decades, this derivation is the least probable.

DINER: *Hey! Where's my chicken tikka masala?*
WAITER: *I'm sorry, sir, it hasn't been invented yet.*

CRYING OUT FOR A CURRY?

Can curry be addictive? A report published by Professor Stephen Gray and a team of researchers at Nottingham Trent University recently aimed to illustrate the point. Commissioned to conduct a survey to see if the introduction of curry in the UK over the last 50 years had produced any physical changes he concluded that curry produces a natural high that makes us crave them more than other foods. While the report stated that: 'the combination of ingredients stimulates more taste receptors on the tongue,' food experts argued that cravings and full-flown physical addiction were entirely different things. The regular curry eaters tested, aged between 10 and 70 years, were said to be 'dazzling their tastebuds to a state of confusion', perhaps something to do with eating several flavours at once, which stimulate several areas of the tongue at once. Apparently the prospect of a tikka masala, elicited a 4.9% rise in blood pressure, compared to only 1.8% rise by traditional British food.

It will surprise most people – old Indians inclusive – to learn that the dish we call curry is not of India, nor, indeed, of Asiatic origin at all. There is reason to believe that curries were first introduced into India by the Portuguese.
Captain Basil Hall, Scottish colonial explorer, getting his Spice Trail history completely back-to-front

BURNING QUESTIONS

Which spice gives some curry its vibrant yellow colour?
Answer on page 151.

THE CULINARY ADVENTURES
OF DEAN MAHOMET

Letter XXVI: *On the tree-groves of Bombay and their produce, encountered circa 1778...*

'The soil of this country is chiefly employed in cocoa-nut groves, palm-trees, &c... As to the cocoa-nut tree itself, not all the minute descriptions I have heard of it, seem to me to come up to the reality of its wonderful properties and use. Nothing is so unpromising as the aspect of this tree; nor does any yield a produce more profitable, or more variously beneficial to mankind: it has some resemblance to the palm-tree; perhaps one of its species. The leaves of it serve for thatching; the husk of the fruit for making cordage, and even the largest cables for ships. The kernel of it is dried, and yields an oil much wanted for several uses, and forms a considerable branch of traffic under the name of copra. Arrack, a coarse sort of sugar, called jagree, and vinegar are also extracted from it, besides many other particulars... The cultivation of it is extremely easy, by means of channels conveying water to the roots, and a manure laid round them, consisting of the small fry of fish, known by the name of buckshaw... There are also here and there interspersed a few brab-trees, or rather wild palm trees; (the word brab being derived from Brabo, which in Portuguese signifies wild) that bear an insipid kind of fruit, about the size of a common pear, and produce from incisions at the top, the toddy or liquor drawn from them, of which the arrack that is made, is esteemed much better than that from the cocoa-nut tree.'

Dean Mahomet, *The Travels of Dean Mahomet,* 1794

AN ODE TO RICE

Say 'curry', and the word you are most likely to get back is 'rice'. From pilau to pish-pash to pre-cooked, rice is the ultimate curry companion. Dished up with nearly all the curries of the world, it is used to soak up sauce, absorb aromas and even comes in perfectly handy where knife, fork, spoon or chopsticks do not exist. India's Mughal rulers used it to create biryani, and, it is said their witty cooks had an influence on modern-day pilau by colouring rice to make it look like jewels. Kedgeree, with a little help from haddock (courtesy of the British love of kippers perhaps), was also born of rice. Unknown to Britain before traders and conquerors embarked on Eastern shores, namely India, it is now a staple of our diets (although risotto aside, it does still tend to accompany Asian-style dishes). In Vietnam and Cambodia, curry comes with sticky rice balls; in Japan it may come in soup; in Malaysia, no street is complete without nasi goreng; in Thailand, red, green or yellow curry is best served with coconut rice – in the shell; in Bali, it is placed on the thumb and used to portion other food into the mouth; and in the jungles of Borneo, one traveller reported the popular pineapple curry to come with an offer of six types of rice, with no one leaving until it was all gone. Plain, fragrant, fried or boiled, we salute you o' humble rice – without you, curry just wouldn't be the same.

PRIVATE THAI

When conceptual and performance artist Rirkrit Tiravanija was commissioned to present a retrospective at the Serpentine Gallery in London's Hyde Park – 5 July to 21 August 2005 – visitors were presented with some very hearty fare. Born in 1961 of Thai parents, the winner of America's prestigious Hugo Boss prize specialises in recreating everyday life. In the Serpentine re-creation of his New York apartment, this included serving up home-cooked dishes for his voyeuristic guests, or indeed letting them loose in the 'kitchen' to cook their own. Fans had access to rice, noodles and curry powder as well as plates, cutlery, cooker, fridge and sink. In other cities the re-creation was open 24 hours a day and like a Big Brother type of experiment, some couples were rumoured to have even used the bed. Tirvanija's work comments on present-day social structures where integration and community is often lost in a wave of fast food. In the spirit of counteraction, he will often pop into his exhibitions or private views to cook up a Thai meal for exhibition pundits: Top of the menu? Thai curried vegetables of course.

On the spice trail and around the world on the good ship Curry...

While eastern African cuisine absorbed a number of flavours from an extensive Indian and west Asian population, 'curry' in sub-Saharan west Africa is a more tentative affair. A recipe for west African Curry may include stewing chicken or beef with tomatoes, onions, coconut, raisins and curry paste. As with many countries, side dishes making full use of native spices and legumes, lend a distinctive 'west African' flavour. Boiled eggs, fried or fresh bananas and plantain, toasted coconut, okra and peanuts are classic accompaniments. Nigeria, Cameroon, Ghana and coastal regions also profess a fondness for very hot food, with chillis imported from the Caribbean. British colonialism also had a hand in establishing 'curry' in countries such as Nigeria, when officers were transferred there from the Raj. While Jollof rice – a typical Nigerian dish – has similarities to biryani (being slow-cooked in a pot with marinated meat), although this is said to originate from the Wolof peoples of Senegal and Gambia.

BRING A BOTTLE

Beer and curry go hand in hand, but let us not forget wine. In a visionary 1938 publication, *Curry Recipes: Selected from the Unpublished Collection of Sir Ranald Martin* by Mrs Jessop Hulton, Martin writes: 'No fine wine can be expected to be happy in the company of curry. Iced lager is considered best, but a Vin Rose or a light white wine, served very cold, should prove acceptable.' Although a man of high regard and worldly tastes by all accounts (he was famous for inviting guests of distinction including Florence Nightingale to partake in his curry feasts) his publishers, the Wine and Food Society, might have had something to do with that. In 1968, Doris Ady, author of *Curries from the Sultan's Kitchen*, seemingly a woman with a taste for *du vin*, wrote: 'I would say that the dry, heavy wines are not suitable to serve with curries. With red meat curries, we like to serve a chilled rose, or any other light, sparkling wine. With fish, shellfish, and the white meat curries, a chilled hock, moselle, or one of the dry sparkling wines. White burgundy, a winner in the wine stakes, is my favourite with almost any type of curry.' Today's wine experts are still divided on the subject of curry and wine. But one man is 'doing a Cobra' – Warren Edwardes' Wine for Spice company proves spicy wine is no longer reserved for Christmas. In fact, some curry houses have a 'bring your own bottle' policy, and corkscrews on hand, that positively encourage you to open the *vin*.

...AND A POPPADUM IN A PEAR TREE

Some alternative ways to spice up Christmas,
inspired by www.curryhouse.co.uk

- **Classic British roast turkey curry**
  A flashback to the days of the Raj – classic curried Christmas
  roast in a sweetened sauce

- **Gajar halwa (Christmas cake with a twist)**
  Warm carrot cake with pistachio, khoya (Indian reduced milk),
  rose water and spicy cardamom

- **Roast turkey shami kebabs**
  Cold turkey spices up nicely to morph into seasonal shami kebabs

- **Turkey jalfrezi**
  Just add onions, peppers and a generous helping of hot
  curry powder

BURNING QUESTIONS

What do the following mean in Thai cuisine?
a) Neung
b) Op
c) Han
Answer on page 151.

A SUDAN RECALL

In July 2005, the Food Standards Agency warned that rogue cancer-causing dye had worked its way into more food products, although a European Commission ruling banned its inclusion in 2003. Curry houses especially were alerted to be on the look-out, and urged to check if their stocks of spices contained the culprit, Sudan I. Reported by some experts to be the biggest food recall in history, some 357 items were on the black list at the time. The agency's actions were prompted when a batch of chilli powder used to make Crosse & Blackwell Worcester Sauce was found to have the food colouring in it. This was then used in other products, sparking an epidemic across the supermarket food chain. Curries, pizzas and even Pot Noodles were either sent back or sent in for testing. Even *Masterchef* presenter, Loyd Grossman wasn't immune. Although testing is now super tough, in 2006, his ready-to-pour red lentil dhansak sauce was reported by the BBC to have been stripped from the shelves, albeit only with very low levels of the Sudanese imposter in. Something to ruminate on.

*Page reference for Thai Sauce (Nam Prik) in Robin Howe's Far Eastern 91
Cookery (1969); it is served as a condiment with curry and rice*

Indian food is so interesting partly because it is so scientific. In anybody's house, no matter in which part of India, every single ingredient that goes in has a reason to be there. Chefs make it sound like an art, so people believe it can't be done, but I think you have to translate it into chemistry. For example, you have to put the spices into hot oil, because the oils in the spices are oil-solvent, and hot oil tends to penetrate and release their flavour and aroma. You have to cook tomato on a low flame, because you want the acid to evaporate, and if you cook it too high, the water evaporates and leaves the acid behind.

Sriram Ayur, executive chef of Keralan restaurant, Quilon, Crowne Plaza St James's, 45-51 Buckingham Gate, London SW1E 6AF, quoted in *The Observer Food Monthly*, 12 May 2002

HOW THE CURRY HOUSE GOT ITS NAME

The 'Passage to India'
In the words of that literary Raj, Rudyard Kipling, some things are 'just so'...

EM Forster's 1924 novel *A Passage to India*, and the 1984 film provided the dramatic inspiration for an influx of curry houses from the mid-1980s. David Lean (of *Doctor Zhivago* and *Lawrence of Arabia* fame) directed the epic, which sparked a nationwide hunger for all things Indian, and a hankering for the exoticism associated with the days of the Raj. However, the theme of both book and film adaptation was somewhat of a more sinister affair. The tale focused on a false accusation of rape against an anglicised young Indian doctor by a white female tourist he unwittingly took to some caves. The plot highlighted turn-of-the-century tensions between Indians and colonial British that were soon to come to the boil. A potent dish of sexual intrigue, interracial relations and alarming Empirical prejudice, captured by Lean's breathtaking cinematography, provided real food for thought for the millions of moviegoers who left cinemas wanting to know more. India's own theatrical backdrop – many of the scenes were filmed in Bangalore – also prompted its voyeurs to book their own passages to Eastern shores. For those who couldn't make it all the way to Asia, Britain paid tribute with a wave of Passage to India curry houses that allowed its diners to at least sample some Anglo-Indian fare. Passage to India restaurants can now be found from Washington to Whitby to a jazzed-up Passage thru' India in Malaysia's Kuala Lumpur.

Elvis might have choked on his last hamburger, but The King is also said to have loved a good curry. *Are You Hungry Tonight? Elvis' Favourite Recipes* is Brenda Butler's tribute to The King, with ginger curry sauce cited as one of his hot favourites. Meanwhile, over in Swansea, one Peter Singh, known for owning a curry house on Waun Wen Road, was so inspired by Elvis, he decided to become him – he even named the restaurant Gracelands. Not one for keeping his passion to himself, the 'Rocking Sikh Peter Singh' was famous for bursting into city centre pubs and 'entertaining' the punters with his antics. He eventually swapped his day job for a life of rhinestones, taking his diamante-clad turban to 11 different countries and establishing his name with such hits as 'Turbans over Memphis' and 'My Poppadum Told Me'. In December 2005, the Zarin restaurant in Ashford Kent, cashed in on his fame with their curried Elvis. In 2006, the Dil-raj in Abingdon did the same, hiring Gary Glen, one of the top five impersonators in England, to spice up the night. But according to south Wales's record label Taffpop, it's Peter who still reigns supreme as The King of curry. Turning down the role of himself in the film *Twin Town* (1997), Peter's fame has now spread so far, he had to 'leave the building' – Taffpop claim the only way you can get hold of him is to leave a message with a certain local curry house. Whether they'll 'deliver it straight away' is another matter...

MRS BEETON'S CURRY WISDOM

Indian Curry-powder (founded on Dr Kitchener's Recipe)

Ingredients: $1/4$lb of coriander-seed, $1/4$lb of turmeric, 2oz of cinnamon-seed, $1/2$oz of cayenne, 1oz of mustard, 1oz of ground ginger, $1/2$oz of allspice, 2oz of fenugreek seed.

Mode: Put all the ingredients in a cool oven, where they should remain one night; then pound them in a mortar, rub them through a sieve, and mix thoroughly together; keep the powder in a bottle, from which the air should be completely excluded.

Note: We have given this recipe for curry-powder, as some persons prefer to make it at home; but that purchased at any respectable shop is, generally speaking, far superior, and, taking all things into consideration, very frequently more economical.

Isabella Beeton – aka 'Mrs Beeton',
***Book of Household Management*, 1861**

SPICE GUYS

On his time in the spice trade of Kinsay (modern Hangchow), a city south of Beijing in the Kingdom of Kublai Khan

You must know that in this city and its dependencies they make great quantities of sugar, as indeed they do in the other eight divisions of this country; so that I believe the whole of the rest of the world together does not produce such a quantity, at least, if that be true which many people have told me; and the sugar alone again produces an enormous revenue. However, I will not repeat the duties on every article separately, but tell you how they go in the lump. Well, all spicery pays three and a third per cent on the value; and all merchandise likewise pays three and a third per cent. But sea-borne goods from India and other distant countries pay ten per cent.

Marco Polo, *The Glories of Kinsay* [Hangchow], c. 1300

QUOTE UNQUOTE

Chillis are supposed to be addictive – they release endorphins in the body, so they give you this feel-good factor.
Shrabani Basu, Indian-born/British-based journalist, author of
Curry: The Story of the Nation's Favourite Dish (2003)

CURRY WARS

Rubbishing the competition

As curry mania spread across the country, it followed that competition between nearby curry houses would become rife. In March 2005, competitive spirit turned into bad feelings and caused a real stink. A story was reported in Lancashire's local news portal in March 2006, that a man had been given 80 hours community service for tipping rubbish outside the doors of a rival Indian takeaway: Irshad Ali, owner of the Curry Cottage, Farnworth, Bolton, was accused of driving the eight kilometres to Kurry Korner in Chorley Old Road to dispose of his garbage. The mess included rotting carcasses, bin liners of leftover food, cooking oil drums and numerous cardboard boxes. Residents wrongly blamed Kurry Korner for the mess, and business was duly affected. Finally, Ali was caught on police surveillance camera in April, unloading bags on Chorley Old Road, and at other spots around town, including Deane Road and Gibraltar Street. Curry Cottage is now closed and Ali is said to be working at another restaurant in Eccles. Hopefully the Kurry Korner has managed to win its customers back.

With echoes of his famous quote, 'You're only supposed to blow the bloody doors off', Sir Michael Caine opened his Indian restaurant in 2004 with no intention of blowing his customers' tastebuds off – or serving classic curry fare such as hot gravy vindaloo. Deya, at 34 Portman Square in London (just around the corner from the location of original curry house the Hindostanee Coffee House) employed head chef Sanjay Dwivedi of Michelin-starred Zaika, and teamed up with former partner Raj Sharma to present healthy yet traditional dishes 'minus the overbearing spicy gravies'. The restaurant opened to critical acclaim, gaining one of London's only Michelin stars for an Indian restaurant. The *Evening Standard*'s food reviewer Fay Maschler even approved, praising the 'thoughtful concept of making a salad of tandoori, lamb and black eye beans, chicken tikka cooked with three glazes including a piercing pomegranate one [and] crunchy green vegetables.' Thanks in part to curry, the Oscar-winning actor looks set to enjoy his salad days.

FLOCK-PAPER FAVOURITES: MADRAS

Deciphering the curry house menu...

One down from the vindaloo in the spice stakes, this red-brown dish is classically medium hot. An Anglo-Indian invention pertaining to one of Britain's empirical power centres, madras (Britain moved their main east-coast base there in 1640) the dish is a classic example of how the 'curry' came into its own. While other dishes could hark back to a particular era or region, culminating spices and techniques along the way, the madras curry followed the template base or formula for Anglo-Indian curries still employed today: simply take a handful of spices – such as ginger, nutmeg, cinnamon, cloves, cardamoms, coriander, cayenne pepper and turmeric; grind to a 'curry powder' with onions and garlic; make a paste with butter or ghee; add the meat and cook. In this form, the madras curry was simply a spicy sauce for meat, made from a spoonful of curry powder, some onions and tomatoes. In WH Dawe's *The Wife's Help to Indian Cookery* (1888) there can be found a recipe for madras karhi where mutton is cooked in this way. Today, much the same mix of spices is used to create the perfect madras. The spicy flavour can be toned down with more tomatoes to cater for curry eaters who like to stay on the safe side of the fence – or chilli-ed up for those who want to take a walk on the wild side.

Heat factor: Hot to trot.

THE ORIGIN OF THE WORD

Many stories exist as to how the dish curry got its name.
Some of them have been less than complimentary...

Indian food consists of some cereal. In the North this is flour, baked into unleavened cakes, elsewhere it is rice grain, boiled in water. Such food, having little taste, some small quantity of a much more savoury preparation is added as a relish. Curry consists of meat, fish, fruit or vegetables cooked with a quality of bruised spice and turmeric, called masala. A little of this gives a flavour to a large mess of rice.

Hobson Jobson (an Anglo-Indian glossary from 1882)

CHUTNEY ON THE SIDE

Why just stick to mango when there are so many variations to try? All are made using unripe fruit or vegetables, unless otherwise specified

Apple chutney

Apricot chutney
(an English variation on the theme)

Aubergine chutney

Coconut chutney

Garlic chutney (made from fresh garlic)

Green chutney (made with coriander)

Guava chutney

Lime chutney

Mango chutney (made from green mangos)

Mint chutney (also known as padina chutney, originated in Punjab)

Onion chutney

Peach chutney

Plum chutney

Prawn chutney (from the Kerala region of India which also
produces a 'dry fish' variation)

Tamarind chutney

Tomato chutney (or green tomato chutney,
made with unripe tomatoes)

The effects of curry abuse were starting to show on Alf and Freda.

CURRIED WORDS

East India Soup

1 large onion
2-3 tablespoons butter
2 large tart apples, peeled, cored, and sliced in quarters
2 tablespoons flour
1-2 teaspoons curry powder
3-4 cups of chicken broth
Salt and pepper to taste
1 cup heavy cream
1 additional apple, peeled, cored, and sliced thin, for garnish

1) Chop the onion fairly fine and saute in butter until limp. Add prepared apples and saute with the onions until almost tender. Stir in flour and curry powder.

2) Stir in chicken broth, and bring to a slow boil. Continue simmering until the apples are soft. Stir in cream and heat, but do not bring to a boil.

3) Taste, and correct seasonings.

4) When hot, float the sliced raw apple slices, each lightly sprinkled with additional curry.

5) Serve hot. Serves six. Note: this is equally good as a cold summer soup.

Catherine Moffat Whipple,
***The Thirteen Colonies Cookbook*, 1975**

YELLOW CURRY NATION

Writing in her 1972 book *The Art of Indian Cooking*, US author Monica Dutt perfectly sums up the 1970s with the line 'Curry – a concoction we are apt to think of as a sort of yellow stew flavoured with curry powder.' Indeed, many Westerners at the time were taken in by food colouring, TV dinners and the bright dawn of 'fast food', and thought it tasted better that way. With her campaign to make curries – and indeed food – more authentic and healthy, Dutt was a forerunner for protagonists such as *Super Size Me*'s Morgan Spurlock, although he proves that curry's fight against fast food is still on today – the Chicken McTikka being a case in point.

BURNING QUESTIONS

Which Indian dessert, made of yoghurt,
shares its name with a canine Hollywood star?
Answer on page 153.

NOT SO HANDI GHANDI

In 2005, Reuters reported that Mahatma Gandhi's family was pleading with the Indian government to force an Australian takeaway firm to renounce its name. Handi Ghandi promised 'Great curries... No worries' but the snappy title was, the Gandhi family said, taking the great pacifist's name in vain. Tushar Gandhi, great-grandson of the revered vegetarian deemed the promotion 'offensive' with meat curries such as beef vindaloo, beef madras, lamb rogan josh and butter chicken on the menu. Of the restaurant he remarked that: 'It goes absolutely against all his beliefs. Using his image to sell beef curries and such doesn't gel.' The restaurant also used a caricature that resembled Mahatma on its advertising and a jingle with a voice that sounded remarkably like Ben Kingsley's portrayal of him in the 1982 hit film *Gandhi*. Troy Lister, owner of the restaurant, was unavailable for comment at the time. He may have one argument in that his 'Ghandi' is spelt differently to the actual man's surname (a mistake often made in the West). A harsher tack would be to use the rumour that Gandhi was said to have once tasted a beef curry on British soil. While training to be a lawyer in London, and enjoying a life of relative privilege before denouncing it in protest of India's colonial occupation, he apparently wanted to know what beef tasted like.

Year in the nineteenth century in which Charles Ranhofer, author of one of the first accounts of curry, left his post as chef at Delmonico's, New York

CURRY-OKE CLASSICS

Musical maestros from a curry house near you...

Bhuna Round the World and I Can't Find My Bhaji ..... Lisa Stansfield

Bhuna to be Wild .... Steppenwolf

Bye Bye Balti .... Bay City Rollers

Chicken Tikka (Chiquitita) .... Abba

C'mon Every Bhaji .... Eddie Cochran

Dansak on the Ceiling .... Lionel Richie

Dansak Queen .... Abba

Girlfriend in a Korma .... The Smiths

Good Thing Goan .... Sugar Minot

I Don't Want to Dansak .... Eddie Grant

Instant Korma .... John Lennon

It's Bhuna Hard Days Night .... The Beatles

Jalfrezi Jalfrezi Nights .... Kiss

King Prawn Masala Drinks Are Free .... Wham

Korma Chameleon .... Culture Club

Love Me Tandoor .... Elvis Presley

Mr Tandoori Man .... The Byrds

Paperback Raita .... The Beatles

Tandoor Deliver .... Adam and the Ants

Things Can Only Get Bhuna .... D:Ream

Tie Me Vindaloo Down, Sport .... Rolf Harris

Tikka Chance On Me .... Abba

Vindaloo .... Abba

We Are Jalfrezi .... Sister Sledge

We Don't Have to Tikka Clothes Off .... Jermaine Stewart

When I Phall in Love .... Nat King Cole

You Can't Curry Love .... Diana Ross and the Supremes

Curried Beef

Ingredients – A few slices of tolerably lean cold roast or boiled beef, 3oz of butter, 2 onions, 1 wineglassful of beer, 1 dessertspoonful of curry powder.

Mode – Cut up the beef into pieces about 1 inch square, put the butter into a stewpan with the onions sliced, and fry them of a lightly-brown colour. Add all the other ingredients, and stir gently over a brisk fire for about 10 minutes. Should this be thought too dry, more beer, or a spoonful or two of gravy or water, may be added; but a good curry should not be very thin. Place it in a deep dish, with an edging of dry boiled rice, in the same manner as for other curries.

Time – 10 minutes.

Average cost – exclusive of the meat, 4d.

Seasonable – in winter.

Isabella Beeton – aka 'Mrs Beeton',
Book of Household Management, 1861

THERE'S NO TASTE LIKE HOME

There's no risk of missing lunch in Mumbai, thanks to a unique system of home food delivery that has been functioning in the city for more than 100 years. Every day, an estimated 200,000 meals are delivered by around 5,000 dabawallas or tiffin carriers for which hungry workers pay an average 325 rupees a month (about £3). Dishes – often a favourite curry – are generally cooked up by the lady of the house – or a hired chef for single folk – and transported in a tiered metal lunch box or tiffin (old English for midday meal). Not unlike an Olympic relay team, the well-oiled procedure involves dabawallas meeting up in railway stations and other agreed points to pass their boxes for the next leg of the run (walk or cycle, depending on the route and the mobility of the man). Carriers use a special code of numbers and coloured string or wires to map and track the tiffins' route. The work delivery service started in 1890, when a Parsee broker working in Ballard Pier (then a distance from the main residential area) employed a young man from Pune to fetch his lunch every afternoon from home. As word caught on, the young man became something of an entrepreneur, carrying as many tiffin boxes as he could. Today, the tiffins find their way to factories, government offices, railway stations and IT plants with 99% accuracy (one error in eight million meals) – in fact, no self-respecting worker would break for lunch without one.

Number of countries where rice in cultivated; it is produced on every continent except Antarctica

GLOBAL WARMING:
WEST INDIES AND THE CARIBBEAN

On the spice trail and around the world on the good ship Curry...

Much of the West Indies was colonised by the British by the early nineteenth century – Guyana joined Jamaica and Trinidad in 1814. Following the abolition of slavery in 1833, John Gladstone, a prolific plantation owner in the region (and father of future British prime minister), secured cheap labour from India. By 1869, Guyana alone had more than 30,000 'free' labourers, many of whom swapped a long and cruel passage home for a plot of land after their contracts ended. They grew sugar cane, cacao, vegetables, and with their native knowledge of rice cultivation, a lucrative new crop that was to become a major export. Drawing on local ingredients to develop their curries, spicy heat was added in Guyana with the wiri wiri pepper, and in Trinidad with the scorching scotch bonnet. Local favourites include bunjay dahl – split peas with browned (as in bhuna) onions, garlic and chilli – in Guyana; Trinidadian curry incorporating local, Indian and Mediterranean ingredients (from Madeira and Malta) including saif (a cross between chives and spring onions), parsley, scotch bonnet, shadow beni and culantro (both similar to cilantro); and, of course the national dish of goat curry in Jamaica – goat being used in the absence of beef – served with rice and peas.

INGREDIENTS IN A MULLIGATAWNY

As found in *The Art of Indian Cooking* **by Monica Dutt. Serves six.**

2 cups grated fresh coconut or unsweetened flaked coconut
2 cups boiling water
3lb fryer (chicken), disjointed, and skinned
1 tablespoon ground coriander
1 teaspoon ground cumin
$\frac{1}{2}$ teaspoon turmeric
$\frac{1}{4}$ teaspoon mustard seed, crushed
8 peppercorns
1 cup boiling water
salt to taste
1 tablespoon vegetable oil
1 onion, chopped
4 cloves garlic, crushed
2 tablespoons lemon juice

Bill found that ordering extra chillis with his chicken murg thaal had enormous fringe benefits.

TEA, CAKES... AND CURRY

From one institute to another: Curries lauded in Norma Macmillan's *The Women's Institute book of 650 Favourite Recipes*, 1980

Curried celery salad
Curried chicken
Curried cream cheese
Curried plaice fillets
Curried pork loaf
Curried prawns
Curried turkey and pineapple salad
Curry and mayonnaise
Curry from the United Provinces

I GET NO KICK FROM CHAMPAGNE

How does an artist go about highlighting the problem of anti-social youths in his local area? He kicks a curry around the town of course. Indeed, Andre Stitt kicked a carton of curry around Bedford on 29 March 2003, as part of a nine-performance project sponsored by the Arts Council. The White Trash Curry Kick – as it was so charmingly called – first involved him parading through Bedford with a brick-loaded hod, dressed in an Italian football shirt. Quite what the local lager louts thought of that is unclear, but the Curry Kick was designed to reflect their behaviour and try and get them to change their habits of a Saturday night. Hopefully, yobs were not inspired by the exhibition, and the streets covered in successive acts of beaten up vindaloo.

QUOTE UNQUOTE

Miserable gits.
Iqbal Wahab, founder of The Cinnamon Club,
on Indian waiters while editor of *Tandoori*
– the resulting outcry forced him to quit

GLOBAL WARMING: SOUTH AFRICA

On the spice trail and around the world on the good ship Curry...

Get-rich-quick crops of native sugar, arrowroot, bananas, coffee, pineapple and tea lured the British Empire to South Africa. From 1860, British colonials opened plantations in KwaZulu-Natal, formerly under Boer control. More than 150,000 indentured Indians came to work the fields, many from the famine-struck regions of Uttar Pradesh and Bihar. Earlier Cape Malays (a group formed by snatched Indonesian and Indian slaves by the Dutch) morphed European dishes into mild curries, pilaffs and the famous babotie – curried minced meat studded with lemon leaves and cinnamon sticks, topped with custard and baked. Shipped over Indians brought a shared, if region-unspecific, passion for spicy food and (free to work their own land after indenture) went on to control the fruit, vegetable and later spice trade for a time. Dishes such as the bunny chow, 'the food of the Indians', were born. At the turn of the last century, this dish, of curry inside a hollowed out loaf of bread served with pickles, was handed out of the back door of Indian restaurants to segregated 'blacks'. South African Red Spice Mixture is the curry powder now found in most local households.

Research does not show that there is anything particular in curries that is making us physically addicted to it. The addiction may be more similar to other kinds of 'natural high' addictions, like gambling, shopping, or internet use.
Dickon Ross, British, food scientist, editor of *Flipside* and former editor of *Focus*

THE CULINARY ADVENTURES OF DEAN MAHOMET

Born in 1759, Dean Mahomet (aka Sake Deen Mahomed) was the first known Bengali to arrive in the UK, and in 1809 opened The Hindostanee Coffee House: the nation's first Indian restaurant. On his way from his native Patna, he described his life and journey in a stream of letters, ostensibly addressed to a Colonel William A Bailie of the East India Company – although Bailie was in fact a fictitious prop for Mahomet's epistolary style.

The letters were published in 1794 under the title, *The Travels of Dean Mahomet, A Native of Patna in Bengal, Through Several Parts of India, While in the Service of The Honourable The East India Company, Written by Himself, In a Series of Letters to a Friend*: commonly shortened to *The Travels of Dean Mahomet*. His narrative – the first written in English by an Indian – provides fascinating insights into his all-consuming culinary education...

Letter II: *On being a guest in the palace of Patna's Raja at age 11, circa 1770...*
'Dancing girls [were] introduced, affording, at one time, extreme delight, by singing in concert with the Music... at another time, displaying such loose and fascinating attitudes in their various dances, as would warm the bosom of an Anchoret: while the servants of the Raja are employed in letting off the fire-works, displaying, in the most astonishing variety, the forms of birds [and] beasts... Extremely pleased with such various entertainment, the Gentlemen sit down to an elegant supper, prepared with the utmost skill, by an Officer of the Raja, whose sole employ is to provide the most delicious viands on such an occasion: ice-cream, fowl of all kinds, and the finest fruit in the world, compose but a part of the repast to which the guests are invited. The Raja was very happy with his convivial friends; and though his religion forbids him to touch many things handled by persons of a different profession, yet he accepted a little fruit from them; supper was over about twelve o'clock, and the company retired...'
Dean Mahomet, *The Travels of Dean Mahomet*, 1794

Some olde curries you may prefer not to take away...

Acid vegetable curry
Ball curry of liver and udder
Beef à la mode
Buns
Delicious curry soup
Forcemeat balls
Gingerbread nuts
Hussanee curry of udder and liver
Kid curry
Long plum pickle
Meat or birds in jelly
Mutton brains and love apples (tomatoes)
Pickled vindaloo
Pink mango fool
Pish-pash
Red herring burta
Round plum pickle
Tapp sauce gravy for made dishes
Tart and pie crusts of soojee
Tyre or dhye

CURRY CRIMES

A spicy flight

With fear of terrorism riding an all-time high, more than 80 passengers on a Singapore Airline flight on 26 June 2006 were held in quarantine for up to six hours when a yellowish powder was found on their bags. The aircraft had previously been used to transport sulphur and spices, and the substance – found when bags were brought out of the hold at Adelaide airport – was thought to be curry powder. While hazardous material crews were brought in to identify the powder (many poisonous powders are yellow, and ricin is off-white), a total of 500 passengers from three international flights were held, in rooms without toilets, few chairs and no water for up to six hours – an ironic turn of events that held each of them prisoner on account of the suspected crime. One passenger even remarked that Osama Bin Laden must have been having the last laugh if 'a bit of powder can shut down an international airport'. Passengers were only allowed to leave when they were given decontamination showers – the powder was eventually deemed to be harmless. Unfortunately, in today's hot political climate, you can never be too careful.

QUOTE UNQUOTE

*[Curried] black rat was a favourite of King Someswara who lived in
the twelfth century in Southern India and wrote a treatise on
kingship which (among other things) detailed the jewels, food and
aphrodisiacs suitable for a king.*
Lizzie Collingham, British, author of *Curry: A Tale of Cooks and
Conquerors*, justifying her inclusion of an unusual recipe

A CURRY ABOVE THE REST

Curry house restaurants voted 'Best in the UK' by Pat Chapman's
Cobra Good Curry Guide between 1991 and 2004 (dates denote
editions of the book)...

1991	Chutney Mary, London SW10
1995	Bombay Brasserie, London SW7
1998	La Porte des Indes, London W1
1999	Chutney Mary, London SW10
2002	Quilon's, London SW1
2004	Madhu's Southall, London

BURNING QUESTIONS

In which country can you eat 'curry bread',
a deep-fried bread filled with curry sauce?
Answer on page 151.

Answer on page 151.

CURRY TO THE RESCUE

Curried lamb or vegetable tikka masala is a comforting option for
British troops posted out to hot war zones such as Iraq and
Afghanistan. The hearty meal is a favourite item in the high calorie
ration packs – dubbed 'rat packs' by its steel-booted squaddies. The
packs are something of a 'united nations' affair with French onion
soup, hot chocolate, bacon and beans, chicken pâté, hot pepper sauce
and fruit dumplings and custard on the menu. Each perfectly
portioned pack is purported to deliver energy for 24 hours. In
September 2005, the rat packs also proved to be a real lifesaver for
victims of Hurricane Katrina in America. Half a million of the calorie-
rich supplies were flown out to the disaster zone in the southern
states. Thankfully, curry provided some spicy relief for the Cajun-
loving folk of Louisiana, until the worst blew over.

The capital's very first curry houses
The Kohinoor, *Roper Street, London W1*

Named after the world-famous Indian diamond that has controversially resided in Britain's crown jewels for more than 150 years (many call for its return to home soil after being 'stolen' by the Raj), this popular institution was launched by a friend of Dharam Lal Bodua (The Shafi's founder), Bir Bahadur. The restaurant was only pulled down as recently as 1978, and when Bir's brothers Sordar and Shomsor joined him from India, the Bahadur clan went on to open Britain's first curry house chain. Kohinoors reached further corners of the UK, with a 'diamond' curry house in Manchester and Cambridge; Brighton, Northampton and Oxford all received their very own Taj Mahals. The Bahadur Empire grew from strength to strength, and its restaurants provided not only training and jobs for the Lascar (seamen) chefs, but also set a new UK trend for opening an 'Indian' on every street corner.

MAKE DO AND MEND

It's often the way that new dishes – or variations on old ones – come with new ingredients. Curry is no stranger to such cause and effect. The Portuguese and British tempered their colonialism slightly, by introducing a wide range of new fruit and vegetables to the subcontinent. Without the potato, there would be no sag aloo. Remove the tomato, and the chutney shelf would be a less interesting place. Relinquish the pineapple and you not only lose one of India's most distinctive fruits, but also a very tasty pineapple curry. Importantly, chilli is thought to have arrived in India from Portugal, too. Likewise, when dishes could not be created as they were back home, native ingredients were used: for the sour vinegar required for vindaloo, native tamarind and pepper, or a coconut hot toddy were brought in. Back on home soil, the first wave of British curry lovers were often forced to go without certain exotic legumes or fruits. They substituted apples and raisins and then took their new concoctions back to India again. In *Caribbean Cooking, a selection of West-Indian dishes* by P de Brissiere, the make-do-and-mend migration of dishes such as curry is much the same. A man with authentic leanings, he dreams of 'yams, cassava, star-apples, grenadilla' soon reaching our shores. While the supermarkets heeded his prophetic fantasy – some say to the detriment of local produce and the environment – the evidence remains that a 'curry' can be made with whatever you have on hand today. Use thy knowledge wisely.

CELEBRITY CURRYS

And the key ingredient of their success
(proving that curry takes and make all sorts)

Adam Curry, *MTV VJ*
Declan Curry, *business journalist*
Edwina Curry, *politician*
John Curry, *Olympic figure skater*
Kid Curry, *bandit cowboy*
Mark Curry, Blue Peter *presenter*
Paul Curry, *magician*
Tim Curry, *actor*

CURRIED WORDS

Everybody had probably drunk between 10 and 20 pints of beer since the first dignified pint in the White Elephant. Two or three would have fallen by the wayside, quite literally; some of the sensible ones would have returned to their wives, but the single guys were hungry. A leader always emerges at a time of crisis. It was the one who stood on the table, pint in hand, tie unknotted, shirt undone, who, bright eyed and sweating, called out 'Who's for the Curry House?' And so, once again, we piled back into the vehicles, more crowded than before because one or two had disappeared, and headed back over the Clifton suspension bridge, down to the city centre, past the bus station and along to Stokes Croft where a flickering yellow neon sign announced the existence of the Koh I Noor Indian Restaurant.

Inside the dining room, with its 14 tables standing on a slightly sticky, thick carpet, each table had a slightly soiled but very starched tablecloth. The walls were covered in tawdry flock and the exhausted waiters, in their stained dinner jackets which were almost a deep, dark green through years of wear, adjusted their clip-on bow ties and prepared for the onslaught. They had an air of resigned acquiescence. Each table was dressed simply with a salt and pepper pot and a stainless steel sugar bowl filled with white sugar lumps. The call was for – because that's all there really was – six chicken vindaloo, nine meat Madras, four plates of evil smelling, deep-fried, crispy Bombay duck and mango chutney and, of course, 15 pints of lager. The bewildered waiter wrote the order on a series of little duplicate pads and headed for the kitchen only to be called back by the blue-eyed fly-half with crinkly blond hair, who was training to be an accountant, and from his position of authority on the main table he would say, 'Make that 30 pints.'

Keith Floyd, *Floyd's India*, 2003

GO GARAM MASALA

Garam meaning 'hot' and masala meaning 'spices' is a common ingredient in curry recipes. But in the presence of curry powder – with its 'title' name – it can fail to get a look in by some aspiring curry chefs. This is a shame as the mixture, originating from those spices used to heat the body in Ayurvedic medicine, can add a more authentic aspect to dishes. This not only comes from the combination of spices, but the fact that they are often thrown in at the end – in traditional Indian cooking, fresh spices were and are added at different points in the process to release their flavours at the optimum time. The main ingredients of the brown, aromatic mix are usually coriander, cumin, black pepper, cardamom, cinnamon and cloves. Some households or commercial mixes add nutmeg and ginger – or use higher proportions of coriander and cumin temper things down. The ingredient that turns curry powder yellow – turmeric – is noticeable in its absence.

HOT LINKS

Get your fill of curry, even when the takeaway has closed...

www.curryclub.org.uk
www.curryguidenet.co.uk
www.curryhouse.co.uk
www.currypages.com
www.madaboutcurry.co.uk
www.patchapman.co.uk
www.londoncurry.co.uk

HOPE FOR THE MORNING AFTER

A report in the *Daily Mirror* on 24 May 1995 gave some credence to curry-loving lager louts' animalistic behaviour: apparently 'a hot curry after a skinful at the boozer could be good for your health'. Experiments by researchers at the University of Singapore on rats found that booze-induced rodents, when plied with the equivalent of several pints of lager on humans, limited the damaging effects of drink when fed with chilli. The study showed that the addition of the hot stuff – namely the chemical component capsaicin – could protect stomach cells against the worst ravages of alcohol. More than 10 years on, the vindaloo is still high on the pub-crawl agenda of many British provinces, although the results of this ongoing national experiment may well render the results of the report unfounded.

**A little help preparing the family menu for the
first three days of your stay…**

Day 1
Clear soup
Roast leg mutton
Harico
Chicken curry
Bread and butter pudding

Day 2
Mulligatawny
Beefsteak pie
Cutlets à la soubise
Kakob curry
Pancakes

Day 3
Vegetable stew
Boiled fowls and tongue
Mutton and cucumber stew
Dry curry
Custard pudding

SUGAR AND SPICE

Chocolate and curry – a strange combination, you might think – but cocoa and chillis have been cuddling up for years in South American recipes (chilli con carne and hot chocolate to name just two) and over in Hawaii. While choice chocolatier Vosges are getting their just desserts from fans of their chocolate truffles, a wave of British curry houses have been coming up with dishes made with chocolate curry sauce. In Wakefield, the chocolate curry is a hit with the locals – comfort indeed for those cold winter nights. In Birmingham, chocolate, spice and all things nice are the perfect ingredients for a comforting korma. But according to the *Asian News*, Manchester's Minara Cook seems to have the market cornered. The daughter of Nazir Ud-Din, founder of the famous Nazir's tinned curry and pickles range, is said to have got the inspiration for her chocolate curry sauce from her own daughter – a combined curry monster and chocoholic. Launched in 2001 to great applaud, the sauce also contains raisins, dates, tamara, garlic, ginger, black pepper and cinnamon – all in all, another sweet success story for the world of curry.

110 *Number of grams, times 10, of lentils consumed by UK chef Nigel Slater in
2002 (from diary published in* The Observer Food Monthly)

CURRY 'N' CHIPS

According to Lizzie Collingham in *Curry: A Tale of Cooks and Conquerors*, it was the Sylheti community who helped to launch the popularity of curry and chips. Where the first Punjabis in America fused their curry with Mexican enchiladas, canny Sylheti seamen (from the Indian area of Sylhet) trained up in the new wave of Indian restaurants in Britain, began to buy up bombed up fish and chip shops after World War II. By the 1950s, fish and chips had joined the ranks of dishes eaten regularly by the nation's working class: roast on Sunday, hash on Monday, cottage pie on Tuesday, hotpot on Thursday, stewed steak and chips on a Friday and fish and chips before Saturday's football game, or indeed any night after the pub. Chinese and Greek immigrants also saw the promise in buying in fish and chip shops. Many simply added their own flavours and cuisines to what was already there. As flavours merged, curry sauce and chips were sold side by side, and a new dish was born.

FLOCK-PAPER FAVOURITES: BALTI

Deciphering the curry house menu…

Trying to get to the bottom of the balti is a contentious issue; the popularity of the dish, however has undisputed appeal and appears on the majority of UK curry house menus, if not actually specialising in the stuff (just try setting yourself the challenge of not finding a balti in Birmingham, for example). Some say the dish originated in the ancient and remotely mountainous North Indian state of Baltistan, now part of northern Pakistan-ruled Kashmir. Others say this story was circulated during the Birmingham balti boom to add authenticity and exoticism to the dish and it actually refers to the two-handled 'balti pan' in which it is cooked. Further still, others argue that the dish originated in Peshawar, north-west Pakistan where the cooking pot and dish is known as *karahai* or *karai*. There are even some who deem a bald cook was in part responsible for the dish's name. Either way, a balti is now taken for a combination of ingredients – often a medium-hot combination of meat, fried green peppers and coriander – that are curried and then brought to the table still cooking in the pan, to be eating cutlery free and mopped up with naan bread (leavened bread). For balti-loving lager louts looking for trouble, the joke may actually be on them: in Hindi, the word 'balti' means cast-iron slop pot or bucket – a waiter-gratifying taste of their own medicine perhaps…

Heat factor: Hot to trot.

The crowd look on in amazement as Jenkins' chilli high kicked in.

QUOTE UNQUOTE

I have been trying to get to the bottom of that one for years.
Peter Grove, co-author of *Curry, Spice and All Things Nice* on the question of who invented chicken tikka masala

GLOBAL WARMING: THAILAND

On the spice trail and around the world on the good ship Curry...

Like Indo-China and Java, Thailand has ancient cultural ties to India that are still present in everyday life today. While no masses of Indian labour were contracted into the country, it is thought that the first Indian Buddhist monks may have brought a taste for 'curry' with them into ancient Siam, as it was then called. Mughal biryani morphed into a similar rice dish, khao moag, with the help of Arab and Muslim Indian traders, while kebabs inspired the popular satay (marinated meat on a stick but with coriander roots, curry powder and soy sauce). The most well-known dish is, however, the Thai curry. In red, green or yellow 'flavours' and varying degrees of strength, native kaffir leaves, holy basil and fresh lemongrass lend that distinctive Thai taste. Traditional Indian curry spices such as cumin and coriander are used sparingly. Add coconut milk, fish sauce and shrimp paste and that hot, sour, sweet taste explodes with tropical aroma.

Thailand has a wide variety of noodle dishes, so it can sometimes be a little difficult to know where to start...

Kuai tiao
rice noodles

Ba mi
wheat and egg noodles

Kuai tiao lat na
wide white noodles with meat and vegetables

Kuai tiao haeng
white noodles flavoured with meat, vegetables and spices

Kuai tiao nam
same as above, but with a broth added

Kuai tiao phat
Thai thin white noodles fried with bean sprouts and meat

Kuai tiao phat si iu sai khai
noodles fried with Chinese sauce, meat, vegetables and egg

Ba mi nam
boiled wheat and egg noodles with broth

Ba mi haeng
same as above but without broth

Ba mi na mu
fried yellow noodles with pork

Ba mi na phak
same as above, but with vegetables

Ba mi krob rat na kung
crisp fried yellow noodles with shrimp

Ba mi krob rat na mu
same as above but with pork

Ba mi krob rat na kai
same as above, but with chicken

Kieo nam wanton
(meat ball) soup

Kieo haeng
wanton with bits of vegetables and spices

Utter the words 'pilchard curry' to fans of the hit 1970s TV show *Abigail's Party* and they could name that show in one. Mike Leigh's TV play revolves around a drinks party thrown by the 'hostess-with-the-mostess' – gin and tonic mainly – Beverly (Alison Steadman). Along with long-suffering husband Laurence (Tim Stern), she invites new neighbours Angela (Janine Duvitski) and Tony (John Salthouse) over, as well as Sue (Harriet Reynolds), the divorcee mother of Abigail – the 15-year-old daughter who is actually throwing the title party next door. Pilchard curry, along with cheese-and-pineapple-on-a-stick is a culinary metaphor for the lower middle class pretensions reflected in the clichéd cuisine of the era. The satirical script drew a massive fan base after the play was aired on TV, and has since gone on to spark a US version starring Jennifer Jason Leigh, and a UK theatre production. One newspaper dubbed the main recipe of the play not pilchard curry, but the 'triumph of material aspiration and lack of identity for people outside of their own desires' (a mouthful in itself). On a lighter note, the dish of the day, branded 'economical' in the play by Angela, found itself at a flurry of Abigail's parties up and down the country, washed down with a grateful G&T and some suitably tacky tittle-tattle.

ORIGIN OF THE SPICES

Turmeric

According to Plant Cultures (a Kew-based charity designed to explore the complexities between the plants and people of Britain and Asia), turmeric probably originated in Western India and can be traced back there at least 2,500 years. The deep orange-red colour is most commonly associated with tandoori and tikka masala dishes, the signature colour of curry powder itself – or as a sprinkling on top of the yoghurt accompaniment raita, Due to its gregarious colour, the plant may have actually been initially cultivated as a dye rather than a spice. Plant Cultures cites it reaching China in 700AD, East Africa in 800AD, West Africa in 1200 and Jamaica in the eighteenth century. Marco Polo raved about it in the thirteenth century, marvelling at its similarity to saffron. While ancient religious Ayurvedic texts such as Sushtra's Ayurvedic Compendium, dating to 250BC, hail it as a spiritual and healing plant, thought to counteract poisoning. When the US won a patent for the healing powers of turmeric in 1995, the Indian government was able to draw on these texts to revoke the decision as part of its Digital Knowledge Campaign. Strangely the US couldn't provide enough sound material for a counter-attack...

TOP OF THE POPP-ADUMS

Side-order sensations from a curry house near you...

Bhaji Trousers .... Madness

I'm a Bhaji Girl .... Aqua

Livin' Dhal .... Cliff Richard

Pass the Chutney .... Musical Youth

Pilau Talk .... Doris Day

Poppadum Preach .... Madonna

Raita Here, Raita Now .... Fatboy Slim

Rice Rice Baby .... Vanilla Ice

Say Aloo Wave Gobi .... Soft Cell

Spice Up Your Rice .... The Spice Girls

Tears On My Pilau .... Kylie Minogue

There's No One Quite Like Naan-Bread .. St Winifreds School Choir

---

MRS BEETON'S CURRY WISDOM

Curried Rabbit

Ingredients – 1 rabbit, 2oz of butter, 3 onions, 1 pint of stock No 104, 1 tablespoonful of curry powder, 1 tablespoonful of flour, 1 teaspoonful of mushroom powder, the juice of $\frac{1}{2}$ lemon, $\frac{1}{2}$lb of rice.

Mode – Empty, skin, and wash the rabbit thoroughly, and cut it neatly into joints. Put it into a stewpan with the butter and sliced onions, and let them acquire a nice brown colour, but do not allow them to blacken. Pour in the stock, which should be boiling; mix the curry powder and flour smoothly with a little water, add it to the stock, with the mushroom powder, and simmer gently for rather more than $\frac{1}{2}$ hour; squeeze in the lemon-juice, and serve in the centre of a dish, with an edging of boiled rice all round. Where economy is studied, water may be substituted for the stock; in this case, the meat and onions must be very nicely browned. A little sour apple and rasped cocoa-nut stewed with the curry will be found a great improvement.

Time – altogether $\frac{3}{4}$ hour.

Average cost – from 1s to 1s 6d each.

Sufficient for – 4 persons.

Isabella Beeton – aka 'Mrs Beeton',
Book of Household Management, 1861

POPPADUMS IN A PICKLE

Fourteen ways to relish your curry – and not a mango in sight:

Aubergine pickle
Aubergine relish
Carrot pickle
Date chutney
Dried shrimp pickle
Fish roe pickle
Green (coconut) chutney
Hot lemon pickle
Lemon pickle
Malabar fish pickle
Mint chutney
Red coconut chutney
Split pea chutney
Tomato chutney

CURRY WARS

Bibles at dawn

In 2003, 'Curry King' Pat Chapman launched a seemingly religious offensive against reigning Queen of the Spice, Madhur Jaffrey. Although united in their passion for curry and food, Madhur crossed camp boundaries when she launched her *Ultimate Curry Bible* with Ebury Press. Pat claimed that the copyright of his groundbreaking epic of 1997, *Pat Chapman's Curry Bible* was being infringed (although no actual copyright was taken out on either title); he was further incensed by Madhur's timing, publishing her testament in July 2003, nearly a year before his gospel was finally republished in May 2004. Pat decided to take the case to court, sure that with the help of a savvy silk (relentless lawyer) he could win his title war. When he realised it might cost him £15,000 a day, and severe damages to his bank balance and his own book title if he lost, he quickly withdrew. Thankfully, King and Queen of Curry still appear together in celebrity chef TV heaven from time to time, and Pat's rage has subsided from scorching phaal to mellow korma over the years. In a review on his website he also acknowledges that Madhur's 'Ultimate' curry bible 'is an excellent book' with an entirely different angle to his own, now 'New' one, although he can't help himself from pointing out a few errors including an 'irrelevant full-stop and some repetition in the text' on page 150. If you want to stop the war, just buy them both.

Over in Australia, in 1968, one Doris M Ady launched curry on her country, in *Curries from the Sultan's Kitchen – Recipes from India, Pakistan, Burma and Ceylon*, along with the introductory statement: 'Visitors from Asia do not come to us in any great numbers, and we in turn have been apt to travel in a westerly direction, rather than to explore the sights and smells of Asia.' Looking back it's hard to imagine an Antipodean not tucking into a Thai curry, or indeed travelling to Asia to explore its shores. OK, Lonely Planet's *Across Asia on the Cheap* (now *South East Asia on a Shoestring*) published in the early 1970s, an influx of chartered flights, and a Commonwealth passport may have had something to do with the increase of intrepid travellers and their culinary preferences over the past 35 years. The influx of Asian immigrants entering Australia after the Vietnam War also added new flavours to the melting pot. But, however curry got there, it certainly tempted the taste buds and prompted the opening of new doors.

QUOTE UNQUOTE

The British invaded India in the nineteenth century with gunpowder.
Now we have come back… and transformed whole swathes of
British society with curry powder.
Sir Gulam Noon, British-based ready-meals tycoon

TALES OF THE TAMARIND

A July 2004 report in *The Times of India* enthused about the cultural crossover of curry, as the stars of *Shrek 2* dined in style at Michelin-starred British restaurant Tamarind – one of the capital's current favourites. Fourteen diners, including such famous names as Antonio Banderas, Melanie Griffith, Steven Spielberg and Eddie Murphy feasted on a spread prepared by top chef Alfred Prasad. Tamarind is also known to have prepared a meal for 100 people, gossipmongers estimate to have cost a hot £40,000. In *The Times of India* report, Prasad proudly attests to have served his authentic cuisine to a stellar blend of guests including the Sultan of Brunei, Tom Cruise, Sharon Stone, Mel Gibson, Nicole Kidman and Chelsea Clinton. Meanwhile *Shrek 2* jumped on the spice bandwagon soon after, with a new range of merchandise using a popular curry spice – sour green tamarind-flavoured Shrek candies.

Door number of the Karwansara restaurant and guesthouse, Interior 117
Ministry Road, Kabul, Afghanistan

Curry in its twentieth century manifestation – a meat or occasionally vegetable stew flavoured with commercial curry powder – is essentially a British dish.
John Ayto, English, author of *The Glutton's Glossary*

ORIGIN OF THE SPICES

Mustard

Mustard has been cultivated in India for thousands of years, but some forms are also indigenous to the Mediterranean and southern Europe. An erect herbaceous plant with beautiful yellow flowers and spicy seedling leaves, it has long been valued for its intense flavours and healing properties. The name 'mustard' comes from the Latin *mustum ardens* or 'burning must'. This stems from the 'must' or unfermented grape juice with which the Romans pounded the seeds to develop their pungent and burning qualities. Seeds come in white, yellow, black or brown – sometimes called Indian mustard – and both whole versions and powdered form has been a classic component of the curry. Indians used it in native dishes before the advent of the dish, as did Middle Eastern cuisines. When these combined with other influences to form curry, the mustard went with them. The leaves and stems of the plant are also added raw to soups and stews, while mustard oil was valued for its role in the pickling process where vinegar was not available. Classic Bengali cuisine is often cooked with the oil, imparting a signature yellow colour and warmth. In Ayurvedic texts, brown mustard seeds are considered a digestive and good for alleviating stomach discomfort and gas, traditionally sautéed in ghee until they pop. Today, the curry house kitchen isn't complete without a generous supply of the stuff and TV chefs seem to love the drama when the popping begins.

BURNING QUESTIONS

Why would you order the following in an Indian restaurant?
Poori
Parantha
Phulka
Answer on page 151.

At the end of his Christmas delivery, Santa liked to load up on curry for his elves

THE LEGEND OF ZORRO

Antonio Banderas, star of recent *Zorro* films, revealed to *The Times of India* in 2004 how he was so desperate for an Indian curry when he got to Britain, he had one delivered to Luton Airport. The curry addict phoned ahead from Madrid and arranged for the takeaway to be dropped off as soon as his plane touched down. The paper alleges he treated himself and more than 40 cast and crew of his then current film *Shrek 2* to 'hara kebabs, aloo tikki, lentils and spinach with tomato chutney, bhalla papri chaat, tandoori-grilled portabella, button and oyster mushrooms, mahi machchi tikka and grilled monkfish marinated with gram flour and aiwain'. Strolling up the green carpet (in honour of the ogre), he apparently couldn't help himself splurging even further on the subject of curry, telling the press just how much he loved the stuff.

DINNER WITH THE RAJ

**Common colonial curries, with main ingredients listed,
so as not to cause embarrassment at the table...**

Curry	Curried...
Bengal curry	Chicken (tender, parboiled)
Bindaloo curry	Rump steak (in small pieces)
Brown Bengal curry	Rump steak (parboiled, in small pieces)
Chicken curry	Fowl (chopped and pounded)
Coconut curry	Coconut (and chicken, jointed)
Cold curry	Veal (knuckle of) or fowl (one large)
Curry toast	Fried bread (rounds of, to spread generously on)
Egg curry	Egg (boiled, quite hard)
Hosseinee curry	Mutton or beef (cold, sliced and skewered)
Kidney curry	Kidneys (beef and sheep's, stewed)
Potted curry	Veal, onion, grated carrot, chopped apple (potted ready for camp or picnics)
Vegetable curry	Potatoes, beans, celery, cucumber, turnips, vegetable marrows (in square blocks), cauliflower (tufts of), tomatoes (in judicious quantity), green peas

FESTIVAL FEVER

Japan has more than a passing passion for curry, but all did not bode well for fans at a village festival in Wakayama, July 1998. In a case that took the nation by storm, Masumi Hayashi, 37, was reported to have laced a Japanese curry with arsenic, leaving four people dead and 63 seriously ill. Detectives found the volunteer caterer was alone with the curry for 15 minutes – ample time to put the poison in. Her husband also ran a fumigation business, which gave her access to the weapon of the crime. Hayashi was also suspected of poisoning friends at dinner parties in order to cash in on health insurance policies she had taken out. Following the accusation, media hype in Japan ran high. Unfortunately the attention was thought to inspire more than 40 copycat cases (Japan never too far from seizing a trend), although curry wasn't implicated a second time.

THE CULINARY ADVENTURES OF
DEAN MAHOMET

Letter VII: *On encountering a Faquir – or hermit – outside Monghere near the Ganges, sometime in the middle of 1771...*

'...he wore a long robe of saffron colour muslin down to his ancles, with long loose sleeves, and on his head a small mitre of white muslin, his appearance was venerable from a beard that descended to his breast... At certain hours in the day, he stretched in a listless manner on the skin of some wild animal, not unlike a lion's, enjoying the pleasure of reading some favourite author. In one corner of the house, he kept a continual fire, made on a small space between three bricks, on which he dressed his food that consisted mostly of rice, and the fruits of his garden; but whatever was intended for his guests, was laid on a larger fire outside the door. When we spent a little time in observing every thing curious inside his residence, he presented us some mangoes and other agreeable fruit, which we accepted; and parted our kind host, having made him some small acknowledgment for his friendly reception, and passed encomiums on the neatness of his abode and the rural beauty of his garden.'

Dean Mahomet, *The Travels of Dean Mahomet*, 1794

KARMA KORMA

In India, Sri Lanka, Thailand, Bali or even down on Brick Lane, it's not unusual to see a bowl of curry and rice standing around in the corner of the house, or being marched up to the temple. In Hindu and Buddhist practice, appeasing 'Them-that-be' often includes making offerings of food. It seems the Hindu gods and goddesses like curry as much as man; only when the deity has had his or her fill can mere mortals settle down to a portion of their own. Special occasions even dictate their own curries – at Diwali, or the Hindu Festival of Light, a chickpea and potato curry is common fare, followed by sweet meats using almonds and pistachios. Likewise, Buddhists help themselves along the road to Nirvana, by giving alms to local monks – often a well-received portion of curry. In Kashmir, the lotus root – the flower of which has become a worldwide symbol of peace and harmony – is even curried and its spiritual and physical properties are said to be cleansing. If curry is one step to salvation, we say dish it up some more.

If curry be the food to finally bridge political, religious and class divide, play on. From fourteenth-century Persian invaders, through European colonialism to present-day army food rations (Israel recently commissioned an Indian food company to supply its troops with curry), from Buddha to Gandhi, curry has seen the best and the worst of mankind. It has travelled to the furthest corners of every continent, collecting creeds, cultures and castes along the way, and throwing them all into one big melting pot. In *Curry and Rice on Forty Plates or the Ingredients of Social Life at 'Our Station' in India*, George Franklin Atkinson, captain of the Bengal Engineers, reflected curry's ability to illustrate the times. Published in 1940, he remarked even then: 'The aspect of the Eastern kitchen is not inviting, nor are its inmates, in their outer man, objects of alluring attractiveness; but sit you at your mahogany, and taste the labour of their hands, and whoever questions that dishes delicious and mouth-watering can be dressed by an Eastern cook, let him come at once to Kabob, and we will prove him what really good things can be got at "Our station".' A bigoted remark at best, things have thankfully moved on since. With curry now a firm favourite at the heart of nearly every nation, there is hope that such a delicious dish will finally be made of the world's differences.

READY, STEADY, COOK

The essential ingredients for a good curry, from a nineteenth-century curry connoisseur, who shall remain at large for fear more of his knowledge should be procured...

the curry powder;
the material curried;
the correct cooking;
the rice.

QUOTE UNQUOTE

Chicken tikka masala is now a true British national dish, not only because it is the most popular, but because it is a perfect illustration of the way Britain absorbs and adapts external influences. Chicken tikka is an Indian dish. The masala sauce was added to satisfy the desire of British people to have their meat served in gravy.
Robin Cook, late Scottish politician

122 *Number of pages in Pat Chapman's* Quick After Work Curries *(US edition)*

CRAVING ON THE CONTINENT

**Menu help for curry addicts who may get the
urge while travelling though Europe**

Country	Curry
Dutch	Kerrie
French	Cari
German	Curry
Greek	Kappu
Italian	Curry
Portuguese	Karil
Russian	Карри
Spanish	Curry

FLOCK-PAPER FAVOURITES: VINDALOO

Deciphering the curry house menu...

Britain was not the only European invader to take over the shores of India. The Portuguese also moved in, most notably colonising the now popular beach resort of Goa. While the British introduced new vegetables and spices to their Empire and succeeded in transforming authentic Indian dishes to their own accord, the Portuguese can be credited with inventing an 'Indian' dish of their own. Taking its name from the two main ingredients 'vinho' meaning wine or wine vinegar and 'alhos' meaning garlic, the vindaloo is a spiced-up version of a traditional Portuguese pork dish, the 'Vinha d'Alho'. To procure the classic sour-hot taste of the Portuguese dish in the absence of vinegar, local tamarind and black pepper were ideal replacement ingredients. Into the pot also went a garam masala of black pepper, cinnamon and cloves. However, the main nouveau ingredient was the chilli pepper, often added in fearless proportions. On British curry house menus the 'vindy' often has potatoes added, when the 'aloo' is wrongly translated from the Hindi for potato. It is also well known for its spicy heat (although not as hot as a phall, boys!) and is widely used as a competitive tool by males seeking to affirm their machismo. Unfortunately the yards of ale that often precede this ritual, question the myth that 'a vindy doth maketh the man'.

Heat factor: Super scorching.

Birmingham council (www.birmingham.gov.uk) urges you not to set foot inside its Balti Triangle until you're well acquainted with the following terms...

Barfi	Fudge-like sweet meat made with pistachios, almond and chocolate
Bhaji	Spicy deep-fried fritter made from onion, mushroom and chicken
Katlama	Pastry filled with mince and deep-fried in vegetable oil
Keema	Mince
Naan	Pancake-shaped bread made with special flour, yeast, milk, sugar and eggs. Usually cooked in a tandoor, but can be griddle cooked
Pakora	Potatoes, onion, flour and spices deep-fried, with chicken or fish
Sharmi kebab	Usually beefburger shaped, made with flour, mince and spices
Sheeskh kebab	Minced lamb, skewer cooked and strongly spiced
Tandoor	Charcoal-burning clay oven used for baking
Tikka	Lamb or chicken pieces marinated in yoghurt and cooked on a skewer

MRS BEETON'S CURRY WISDOM

Curried Veal

Ingredients – The remains of cold roast veal, 4 onions, 2 apples sliced, 1 tablespoonful of curry powder, 1 dessertspoonful of flour, $\frac{1}{2}$ pint of broth or water, 1 tablespoonful of lemon-juice.

Mode – Slice the onions and apples, and fry them in a little butter; then take them out, cut the meat into neat cutlets, and fry these of a pale brown; add the curry powder and flour, put in the onion, apples, and a little broth or water, and stew gently till quite tender; add the lemon-juice, and serve with an edging of boiled rice. The curry may be ornamented with pickles, capsicums, and gherkins arranged prettily on the top.

Time – $\frac{3}{4}$ hour.

Average cost, exclusive of the meat, 4d.

Seasonable: from March to October.

> Isabella Beeton – aka 'Mrs Beeton',
> *Book of Household Management*, 1861

CURRY ASIDE

Nine things one '35-years resident' of the Raj deemed 'worth knowing', from *The Indian Cookery Book: A Practical Handbook to the Kitchen in India*. None have anything to do with curry.

How to make stale bread fresh
How to select and keep coffee
How to make lettuce salad
How to substitute for cream in tea or coffee
How to protect bed linen and curtains from burning
How to prevent the smoking of a lamp
How to make transparent paper
How to take impressions of leaves
How to take impressions of leaves on silk

BURNING QUESTIONS

What is a 'thali'?
Answer on page 151.

ORIGIN OF THE SPICES

Chilli

The spice most often associated with curry, chilli – red, green or powdered – was not in fact indigenous to India or Asia, as many would assume. When Christopher Columbus set off west for the 'spice islands' in 1492, in order to open up a direct sea route to China and the treasures it also held, he famously mistook the Caribbean for the outer reaches of the Indies. In a letter written back home he spoke of food 'heavily seasoned with hot spices', pointing the finger at a plant he mistakenly called the 'pepper of the Indies'. In fact, the plant was aji, a form of hot capsicum that the American peoples had been cultivating for over 5,000 years. While the fruits of all capsicums have wrongly come to be known as peppers – the two are in fact unrelated – the Aztec name 'chilli' stuck when the Spaniards came across a similar plant in Mexico. The hot 'fruit' was well received by spice-loving Asian nations such as India, who had been cooking with long pepper (native to Bengal) and black pepper (as we use in the West) for years. Thought to have arrived with or just after the entry of Portuguese explorer Vasco da Gama in Goa, the chilli was soon cheaper than the long pepper and eventually supplanted it. As man came and conquered, so chilli also made its way across the trading posts and into the curries of the world.

If you've ever thought that the one thing that Japan was missing was a Curry Museum, then you need fret no longer. Yokohama Curry Museum opened its doors to curry enthusiasts in January 2001.

Containing seven different curry restaurants, the museum is much more than simply an exhibition of curry's history; it's a full-on onslaught of the senses. The queues are legendary, but there's plenty to occupy yourself with when you're sitting down to eat, including did-you-know facts, such as the date curry was first eaten in Japan by Indian traders (1863, they didn't leave the port) and the date curry was formerly introduced to the Japanese table (1872). There's also an exhibition focusing on traditional accompaniments, including 'dosa', the Japanese equivalent to chapatti or naan bread, plus an interactive spice test and even a room showing old TV ads for curry sauces.

You can find the Yokohama Curry Museum at 1-2-3 Isezakicho, Naka-ku, Yokohama-shi, Kanagawa-ken.

FLOCK-PAPER FAVOURITES: DHANSAK

Deciphering the curry house menu...

Originally a celebratory Parsee dish (Parsee refers to the community of Persian origins that settled down the west coast of India, especially in Bombay), the British curry house well and truly bastardised it when they put a pineapple on top – now the most recognisable feature. The *dhan* stands for rice or lentils while the *sak* relates to the greens or vegetables and the two now combine with chilli, sugar and lemon juice plus spices to create a hot, sweet and sour dish with contrasting flavours and a defined puréed dahl-type texture. Most British curry houses now use masoor dahl (split red lentils) to create the signature sauce, but in some places chana dahl suffices. In *Curry: A Tale of Cook and Conquerors* by Lizzie Collingham, the dish is described as 'a dhal of four pulses which is made with either chicken, mutton or vegetables. It is thick and very spicy, and is best eaten, Parsee-fashion, with caramelised brown rice and fried onions'. In Madhur Jaffrey's *A Taste of India*, Gujuratis added tamarind and jaggery (unrefined sugar from the cane) to satisfy their love of sweet and sour cooking. The dish was a firm favourite on early Anglo-Indian menus, and still hits the spot in British curry houses and on supermarket chain ready-meal menus today.

Heat factor: Mild and mellow.

Two days on from his first madras,
Simon was still recovering.

TWO PINTS OF LAGER AND…

Curry and lager have been long-standing partners on the British scene. Geraldine Bedell tried to get to the root of the 'mysterious' tradition in an article for *The Observer* in 2002 with a story from Namita Panjabi, now part-owner of chic curry house Veeraswamy. He had been told that: '…the King of Denmark came [to Veeraswamy] whenever he was in the country. Frustrated at not being able to drink Carlsberg – which wasn't then available here – he shipped over a barrel, so that when he came to eat it would be available for him. And so began a great, or not so great tradition.' The 'not so great', of course refers to the post-pub lager louts who bring terror to tandoori houses all over the UK (you know who you are). Cobra Beer is now a firm favourite on the curry scene with its motto: 'The beer from Bangalore that lets you eat more… curry!'. As tribute to the winning combination, and its launch into the all echelons of society, Karan Bilimoria, the man responsible for shipping Cobra over to British soil, was recently appointed as a non-party political peer to the House of Lords.

BRUCIE'S BIG CURRY GAFF

Bruce Forsyth certainly didn't play his cards right when invited to a recent Oxford Union debate. Newspapers had a field day bringing down the veteran presenter when he told an ill-received joke about Indian takeaways. He shocked students by taking a mobile phone from an Asian member of the audience – Taski Ahmed – and ordering a curry from her mum who was on the other end of the line. Bruce was prompted to play the joke when Ahmed's phone rang during his speech. Despite her protests that her Bangladeshi mum spoke no English, Bruce grabbed the handset and barked: 'One chicken korma?' When her phone rang again, later in his speech, he followed with the remark: '...and some poppadums.' A wave of nervous laughter did ripple though the hall, but the 'racist comment' prompted some students to walk out in protest. Ahmed appeared to take the comment in good humour, meeting up with Bruce after the speech so he could apologise for any offence caused by his off-the-cuff retort. To Ahmed's older brother, Taneem, however, Bruce and his humour were as outdated as *The Generation Game*.

JOIN THE CLUB

Who can lay claim to the title of 'founder of the original Curry Club'? Rupees at the ready. Place your bets here...

The Curry Club was founded by Pat Chapman aka the 'Curry King' in January 1982, when the grub was still a relative dot on the landscape. With family roots in Indian soil since 1730, Pat deemed that the 'food was literally in my blood' and inherited a deep-rooted interest in spicy food, in particular, curry. Professing more than just a balti bucket's worth of interest in the spice of life – he has been applauded with the credit of actually 'baltifying Britain' – Pat turned curry into a full-time career. Egged on by request from friends for recipes, ingredient sources, and indeed curry tastings, one project included setting up his Curry Club, aided by his wife Dominique. Since then, over 30,000 like-minded curry-holics have joined the club. As Pat professes, his list of discerning luminaries includes: 'lords and ladies, knights-a-plenty... actresses, politicians, rock stars and sportsmen... an airline, a former Royal Navy warship, and a hotel chain... from every continent... from teenage to dotage... from high street traders to high court judges.' No sign of a revolutionary Curry Political Party yet (although Edwina infiltrated the ranks to some point, if only by surname), although Pat and his all-encompassing fan club look set to take over the world. You can, register your vote for Pat's Curry Club at www.patchapman.co.uk.

Number of pages in Kris Dhillon's 1995 publication, The Curry Secret: Indian Restaurant Cookery at Home

CHEF'S ORDERS

The top five curries – or indeed where to find them – as chosen by Atul Kochhar (of restaurant Benares), Britain's first Michelin-starred Indian chef, *The Observer Food Monthly*, July 2006

Lahore Kebab House, 2 Umberston St, Whitechapel, London E1, 020 7481 9737

Sarkhel's, 199 Replingham Rd, London SW18, 020 8870 1483

Mem-Saab, 12 Maid Marian Way, Nottingham, 0115 957 0009

Spice Merchant, 33 London End, Beaconsfield, Buckinghamshire, 01494 675474

Gurkha Kitchen, 111 Station Rd East, Oxted, Surrey, 0883 722621

QUOTE UNQUOTE

Of course! Lager! The only thing that can kill a vindaloo!
Red Dwarf: Lister (Craig Charles) works out how to destroy a curry monster in the season four episode, 'DNA'

CURRIED WORDS

The Marks & Spencer statistics are awesome: the store declares that: 'As a nation we eat 10 packs of M&S curry every minute of the day – that's enough portions in a year to give one to each of the nine million people who live in Bombay.' The store also concludes that:

● Britain's favourite Indian meal is chicken tikka masala – M&S sells 18 tons of it each week.

● M&S sells enough rice each year to tip 140 elephants off the scales.

● The curry suppliers to M&S use an astonishing three-quarters of a million garlic bulbs each year.

● If all the packs of M&S chicken tikka masala eaten in a year were laid end to end, they would stretch from London to Birmingham and back.

● M&S uses enough cream and yogurt a week in its Indian dishes to fill an Olympic size swimming pool.

● The hotter the better is how the Brits like their curries – the fiery piri piri is a distinctive Goan recipe which is now one of the most popular produced by M&S.

Shrabani Basu, on Marks & Spencer product figures,
Curry: The Story of the Nation's Favourite Dish, 2003

Cloves

Another 'C' spice found in curry powder and garam masala, cloves derive from the myrtle family and the botanical name *Carophyllus aromaticus* derives from the latin word *clavus*, after the nail-shaped appearance of the dried clove bud (the word clove stems from *clou*, the French word for nail).

Originating from the Molucca (spice) Islands – now part of Indonesia – Madagascar, Sri Lanka, Malaysia and Brazil are also producers, with Zanzibar (Tanzania) now hailing as one of the biggest exporters since the British introduced clove plantations in the 1800s. Ancient texts such as those from the Han Dynasty (207BC to 220AD) show that China has been importing cloves for at least 2,500 years. Rather than a flavour for food, however, they were using the clove's fragrant properties as a body and mouth deodoriser, much as seventeenth-century Britons used the refreshing fragrance of the citrus fruit to scent their pomanders.

Arab traders were thought to have brought cloves to Europe around 4AD; with the introduction of Persian cuisine and customs to India in the fourteenth century, also came the use of cloves in cooking, creating inter-continental spice mixtures that would form the base of many modern-day curries and their side dish accompaniments.

GLOBAL WARMING: FIJI AND THE PACIFIC ISLANDS

On the spice trail and around the world on the good ship Curry...

When Captain Bligh of *Mutiny on the Bounty* fame recorded the Pacific islands in the late 1700s and following the discovery of sandalwood, Western traders rushed there in the hope of making their fortunes. Fiji came under British rule in 1874 and with them came exotic fruits and spices from the Americas and Africa, plus of course the seemingly never-ending supply of indentured Indian labourers – over 60,000 of them before the practice was abolished – to work the lucrative sugar plantations. They brought the cultivation of pulses and their native spicy and 'curried' cuisine. Over 40% of the population of Fiji is now of Indian descent with chicken, vegetables and tinned fish getting the curry treatment; roti (a thin Indian bread) parcels of curry are now common fare. Despite curry's popularity, recent coups there in 1987 and 2000 signal civil unrest between native and 'non-assimilating' Indian communities – although journalists claim that coup instigator George Speight and his team have been known to tuck into a good curry.

130 *Number of dishes from the most popular area of India, found in Madhur Jaffrey's curry classic,* Flavours of India

LOCATION OF INDIAN RESTAURANTS IN THE UK

Area	No	No 2002	UK population
London/South East	45.6%	45.9%	30.5%
South West	6.5%	6.1%	8.3%
East Anglia	2.5%	2.4%	3.6%
Midlands	16.4%	15.9%	16.2%
Yorks	6.7%	6.8%	8.6%
North West	8.4%	9.7%	11.0%
North	3.0%	2.8%	5.3%
Wales	3.4%	3.3%	5.0%
Scotland	6.6%	6.4%	8.8%
Northern Ireland	0.7%	0.61%	2.7%

(Source: www.menu2menu.com)

FLOCK-PAPER FAVOURITES: ROGAN JOSH

Deciphering the curry house menu...

With its origins in the now disputed region of Kashmir, rogan josh is literally translated by some as 'red lamb', thought by some to stem from one of the main ingredients, red chillis. Other translations of the name refer to the Persian or Urdu word *roghan* as meaning 'oil' or 'clarified butter' (perhaps referring to the cooking method where a stew of meat is cooked in butter at an intense heat) and josh, cited as either a variation of *gosht* meaning 'meat' or literally as 'hot'. In Kashmir the dish is flavoured with regional spices, which vary according to the religion and specific location of the cook. For example, where Hindu Brahman castes traditionally avoid meat for its impure associations, Kashmiri Brahmans add meat but avoid other such 'impure' ingredients such as onions and garlic. They add flavour with ginger or fennel seeds (a regional specialty) and asafoetida instead. The Muslim version may use lots of garlic and the dried flower of the cockscomb plant, a red flowered indigenous plant of Kashmir, to which some historians attribute the red colour. Both in traditional and British versions of the cuisine, however, this is meant to be one hot dish, although the chilli factor can be tempered down for the faint-hearted with other red ingredients – tomatoes and peppers – plus fresh coriander and cream. Check ingredients with the kitchen first or order at your peril.

Heat factor: Super scorching.

Letter XXVII: *On the gathering of sugar, recorded while in Bombay circa 1778...*

'The sugar plantations employ thousands of the natives, who alone, inured to the excessive heat of vertical suns, are adequate to the fatigue of this laborious business. The cane commonly shoots up to the height of five or six feet, and is about half an inch in diameter: the stem or stock is divided by knots, above the space of a foot from each other: at the top, it puts forth a number of green leaves, from which springs a white flower. The canes, when ripe, are found quite full of a pithy juice, (of which the sugar is made) and being then carried to the mill in bundles, are cut up into small pieces, and thrown into a large vessel much in the form of a mortar, in which they are ground by wooden rollers plated with steel, and turned either by the help of oxen, or manual labour; during this process, a liquor issues from them, which is conveyed through a pipe in the vessel above described into another in the sugar-house, and thence passes into a copper, that is heated by a slow fire, so as to make it simmer; it is then mixed with ashes and quick lime, in order to separate the unctuous parts, which float upon the surface in a thick scum, that is constantly taken off with the skimmer. After this, it passes through a second, third, fourth, and fifth boiler, which last brings it to the consistence of a thick syrup. In the sixth boiler, it is mixed with a certain quantity of milk, lime-water and allum, and receives its full coction, which reduces it to almost one-third of its first quantity. It is finally put into small baskets, where it remains some time to cool, and, afterwards, becomes fit for immediate use.

This is the manner of preparing the East Indian loaf sugar, so much esteemed in London, and confessedly allowed to be the best made in any part of the world.'

Dean Mahomet, *The Travels of Dean Mahomet,* 1794

QUOTE UNQUOTE

Among the Indians at a banquet a table is set before each individual... and on the table is placed a golden dish, in which they first throw boiled rice... and then they add many sorts of meat dressed after the Indian fashion.

Megasthenes, from the Anatolian Peninsula (now the Asian part of Turkey), third-century BC author of *Indica*, making one of the earliest known literary references to curry

SPICE ON SCREEN

Mirch Masala (1985)
A Touch of Spice (1989)
Masala (1991)
Mississippi Masala (1991)
Spice World (1997)
Old Spice (1999)
Sugar & Spice (2001)
Cinnamon Hill (2004)
Chicken Tikka Masala (2005)
Garam Masala (2005)
Cinnamon (2006)

ORIGIN OF THE SPICES

Ginger

A native of both India and China, the name of this pungent, often antler-shaped spice is thought to have etymological roots in the Sanskrit word *stringa-vera*, roughly translated as 'with a body like a horn'. Although ginger is often referred to as 'ginger root', the raw form we know so well is actually a rhizome – a thickened stem that grows underground. The plant is mentioned in the Koran, as a way to flavour drinks, by Confucius, and in the *Karma Sutra* where it is hailed as an aphrodisiac. King Henry VIII even commissioned its use to help fight the Plague. A stalwart spice, ginger has shown itself as a constant companion to global kitchens and dining tables for thousands of years. Both Indian native use and imported recipes from the Middle East and Europe dictated that ginger would dig its rhizomes firmly into the world of curry: onions are fried in it; meat is marinated in gingered-up yoghurt; lemon juice and garlic are combined with it to make a base paste; it is sweetened with sugar or pickled with tamarind or vinegar; and the powdered form is often used to add an extra warm zing to garam masala. In Kerala, where the word ginger is thought to stem from the Malayalam (the native tongue of the region) word *inchi* or *inchi-ver* which means 'root', no festival would be complete without inchi curry – a spicy ginger side pickle.

THAI FOOD SUPERSTITIONS

In Thailand you should never...

Eat before your elders...
you will be reborn as a dog

Eat cold rice with hot rice...
you will lose your way easily the next time you go out

Eat food without rice...
you will get rickets

Eat salt under a tree...
the tree will die

Eat the leftovers from your children...
your children will grow up naughty

Eat before a monk... *you will become a bad ghost*

Eat corn when you have the flu... *it will give you a higher fever*

Eat egg when you have cut yourself... *it will make it worse*

Eat all of the rice during your evening meal...
you should leave some for the elves

Eat chicken feet... *it will give you bad handwriting*

Eat other people's food without permission...
it will make your throat swell

Eat chilli sauce in the mortar bowl...
you will give birth to a child with big lips

Eat turtles... *it will make you walk slowly*

Eat dog... *the dog's spirit will possess you*

(Source: Boran Oo-bai *by Sanom Krutmeuang)*

QUOTE UNQUOTE

*I believe very strongly that you can present Indian food any way
you want to, but you can't lose the identity of the cuisine – a rogan
josh has to be a rogan josh. Certain people are trying to confuse.*
Rajesh Suri, general manager of gourmet Indian restaurant
Tamarind, 20 Queen Street, Mayfair, London W1J 5PR, quoted in
The Observer Food Monthly, 12 May 2002

---

134 *Door number on Wokingham Road, Reading, for The Garden of Gulab,
awarded four cobras by online bloggers Naan Trek*

Pete hoped the neighbours wouldn't notice him testing his latest vindaloo sauce

CURRIED WORDS

A former governor of Bombay discusses what the upper classes ate

The upper classes, at least the Bramin part of them, have very little more variety [than the lower]; it consists in the greater number of kinds of vegetables and spices, and in the cookery. Asafoetida is a favorite ingredient, as giving to some of their richer dishes something of the flavour of flesh. The caution used against eating out of dishes or on carpets defiled by other castes gives rise to some curious customs. At a great Bramin dinner, where 20 or 30 different dishes and condiments are placed before each individual, all are served in vessels made of leaves sewed together. These are placed on the bare floor, which, as a substitute for a tablecloth, is decorated for a certain distance in front of the guests with patterns of flowers, etc., very prettily laid out in lively-colored sorts of sand, spread through frames in which the patterns are cut, and swept away after dinner. The [lower-caste] Hindus eat meat, and care less for their vessels; metal, especially, can always be purified by scouring. In all classes, however, the difference of caste leads to a want of sociability. A soldier, or any one away from his family, cooks his solitary meal for himself, and finishes it without a companion, or any of the pleasures of the table, but those derived from taking the necessary supply of food. All eat with their fingers, and scrupulously wash before and after meals.

**Elphinstone, Mountstuart,
*Indian Customs and
Manners*, 1840**

How to 'curry favour' on an international scale

Albania	*ia kreh bishtin dikujt*
Hungary	*igyekszik magát behízelegni valakinek*
Romania	*cāuta sā intre în graţiile cuiva*
Serbo-Croatia	*ulagivati se*
Spain	*congraciarse con*
Sweden	*ställa in hos*
Turkey	*yaranmaya çalışmak*

HOW THE CURRY HOUSE GOT ITS NAME

The 'Rajpoot'
In the words of that literary Raj, Rudyard Kipling,
some things are 'just so'…

A Rajpoot or Rajput is a member of the dominant Hindu military caste in northern India, stemming from the days when the warrior race of Rajasthan was employed as protectors of the Mughal Empire. For visitors to establishments of the same name, the banner implores a distinguished restaurant with upper-class leanings, although military sidelines are hopefully off the menu. Famous UK Rajpoots include Ahmed Chowdury's prestigious Bath institution, opened in 1980. The restaurant is divided into three parts: The Old India, India Cottage and Kamra each with its own character, and the food is a mixture of tandoori, Mughali and Bengali (the latter being not quite Rajasthan, but we'll let award-winning Chowdury off for helping to upgrade the image of British Indian restaurants for more than 25 years). The welcome on Bath's Rajpoot website, www.rajpoot.com, proudly states: 'we are convinced the results would have been endorsed by the Mughal Emperors and will we trust, by the visiting Naswabs, Rajahs and Maharajas.'

Nearby in Bristol another Rajpoot declares that dining in its restaurant: 'is like stepping back in time to the days when India stood for all that was best in British service and excellence'. Over in Birmingham, the Rajpoot – formerly known as the Everest – claims to be the: 'first Indian restaurant in the area back in the 1970s'. With pride obviously riding high in the Rajpoot ethos, don't settle for second best. If your local Raj doesn't make the grade, remind the owner of what his curry house stands for, and complain.

CURRIED THINKING

Illuminating what he thought to be the source of cinnamon

[The Arabian] manner of collecting the cassia is the following: They cover all their body and their face with the hides of oxen and other skins, leaving only holes for the eyes, and thus protected go in search of the cassia, which grows in a lake of no great depth. All round the shores and in the lake itself there dwell a number of winged animals much resembling bats, which screech horribly, and are very valiant. These creatures they must keep from their eyes all the while that they gather the cassia. Still more wonderful is the mode in which they collect the cinnamon. Where the wood grows, and what country produces it, they cannot tell only some, following probability, relate that it comes from the country in which Bacchus was brought up. Great birds, they say, bring the sticks which we Greeks, taking the word from the Phoenicians, call cinnamon, and carry them up into the air to make their nests. These are fastened with a sort of mud to a sheer face of rock, where no foot of man is able to climb. So the Arabians, to get the cinnamon, use the following artifice. They cut all the oxen and asses and beasts of burden that die in their land into large pieces, which they carry with them into those regions, and place near the nests: then they withdraw to a distance, and the old birds, swooping down, seize the pieces of meat and fly with them up to their nests; which not being able to support the weight, break off and fall to the ground. Whereupon the Arabians return and collect the cinnamon which is afterwards carried from Arabia into other countries.

Herodotus,
The Histories, Book III,
c. 430 BC

QUOTE UNQUOTE

Curry – the best comes from India. An imitation is made of one ounce of coriander seeds, two ounces of cayenne, a quarter ounce of cardamom seeds, one ounce salt, two ounces turmeric, one ounce ginger, half an ounce of mace and a third of an ounce of saffron.
Charles Ranhofer, legendary French chef, revealing his favourite spice blend in *The Epicurean*

CURRIED THINKING

This seventeenth-century recipe proves how well English cookery adapted to the use of spices. Thanks to a low quota of strange, old-school ingredients (only 'ale barm' sticks out as obviously antique), it even looks fit to try out in your own kitchen. Besides, it's always worth remembering that spices can use their powers for savoury... or for sweet!

To make spice cakes:
To make excellent spice cakes, take half a peck of very fine wheat flour; take almost one pound of sweet butter, and some good milk and cream mixed together; set it on the fire, and put in your butter, and a good deal of sugar, and let it melt together: then strain saffron into your milk a good quantity; then take seven or eight spoonfuls of good ale barm, and eight eggs with two yolks and mix them together, then put your milk to it when it is somewhat cold, and into your flour put salt, aniseeds bruised, cloves and mace, and a good deal of cinnamon: then work all together good and stiff, that you need not work in any flour after; then put in a little rose-water cold, then rub it well in the thing you knead it in, and work it thoroughly: if it be not sweet enough, scrape in a little more sugar, and pull it all in pieces, and hurl in a good quantity of currants, and so work all together again, and bake your cake as you see cause in a gentle warm oven.

Gervase Markham,
The English Hus-Wife, 1615

BURNING QUESTIONS

Which Thai drink is the most traditional accompaniment to curry?
Answer on page 151.

QUOTE UNQUOTE

Customers have sometimes told me it is not bright red. I tell them I could make it bright red but it would not be good for them. It artificially camouflages meat and makes it look unnatural. Food should not be a fluorescent colour: shine a torch on it and it gleams back.
Cyrus Todiwala, proprietor of Café Spice Namaste in east London, on the dangers of chicken tikka masala

---

FANTASY TAKE-OUTS

The characters of 10 of the artists at the Port Eliot Lit Fest 2006, and what they would have ordered from the curry house if they could only have found their way out of the Diamond Maze...

Dorothy from Rio	Sag aloo, peshwari naan, prawn korma
Duncan Bowie	Poppadums (12), prawn bhuna, garlic naan, mango lassi
Grensal	Thai green curry (very, very hot), plain rice
Hetal	Chicken balti, pilau rice
Little Red Riding in da Hood	Sag aloo, plain naan, raita, chana dahl
MC Hatter	Chicken tikka masala
Queen of Diamonds	Thai green curry (extra hot), coconut rice
Robert O'Brien	Chicken jalfrezi, pilau rice, garlic naan, raita
Samba-rella	Malaysian fish head curry
Snow White and her Seven Deadly Sins	Tandoori chicken, pilau rice, peshwari naan

---

CURRY CRIMES

The Bangladeshi drug baron

In May 2006, *The Observer* reported on a story that would shake the spice world – the chairman of one of Bangladesh's most respected companies has been arrested on suspicion of trafficking huge quantities of heroin in the UK. Badruddoza Chowdhury Momen, chairman of BD Foods Ltd and named Bangladesh's most 'commercially important person' for three years in a row by its grateful government, is alleged – along with six of the same government's officials – to have smuggled his 948 kilograms of 'golden brown' into the country over 15 years, with consignments of food, floor tiles and beauty products. Renowned for supplying spices to Britain's curry houses, one can only wonder whether any of the dope ever reached the food. It is after all, customary to fall into a heavy food coma after a trip to the takeaway, and some people even claim curry gives them lucid dreams. The case continues, but Momen and his associates look set to swap their life of spice vice for a lifetime of porridge.

HOW TO MAKE A LASSIE

There's no point making a curry, if you can't manage a lassie...

Ingredients:
3 cups plain yoghurt
3-4 ice cubes
1 teaspoon salt or 3 teaspoon sugar (depending on whether you want
your lassie to be sweet or salty)
Water

Method:
Crush the ice cubes in a blender with the yoghurt, water and salt/sugar.
Serve chilled or with fruit purée to taste.

CURRY: A CELEBRATION

If you're serious about curry, then the Brick Lane Festival, in
London's East End, is the place to be in early September. More than
60,000 culture and curry enthusiasts descend on the street every
10 September for a spicy mix of food, history and tradition.

Great curry is the foundation for the festival, and the lane's
numerous curry houses expand onto the street to showcase their
mouthwatering dishes. There's plenty to keep you occupied while
you're tasting their wares: there are funfair rides for the kids, live
music performances and plenty of street entertainment. But you
don't have to wait until September to try them out; Brick Lane and
its surrounding area has over 40 different curry houses to try.
Aladin's (well known for its balti dishes) and The Shampan (as
recommended by Pat Chapman in his *Good Curry Guide*) are a
great place to start, but with competition so hot, you can't really go
wrong. The secret is to take a peak through the window to see how
many people are inside. Find the full list on
www.visitbricklane.com.

LET THEM EAT CAKE
(OR AT LEAST, SOME MORE RICE)

In all this rush to stock up on the spicy stuff, how many people
remember to try out a traditional curry house dessert? An enduring
favourite is the kheer, a traditional Indian rice pudding with nuts
and raisin, enriched by cinnamon and cardoman.

140 *Number of 'inspirational' recipes in Monisha Bharadwaj's book* Stylish
Indian in Minutes *(2002)*

My grandmother made endless delicious dishes with coconut; soupy lentils, a wonderful chutney, and peerless bean curry with coconut and mustard seeds.
Padma Lakshmi, Indian model, actress
and wife to Salman Rushdie

HOW WE CAME TO BE TALKING ABOUT THAI

Food is not just about ingredients, temperatures and ingestion. It's the most embodied form of cultural history: it sits before our eyes and nostrils telling us about our influences and prejudices in a very immediate way. And nothing is more telling than the fusions and cross-pollinations which occur within and between cuisines. Thai food was perhaps to 1990s Britain what Elizabeth David's Mediterranean innovations were in the 1950s – new flavours and styles of eating which were met with delight by many, suspicion by some and distress by a few.

These days, there are over a thousand Thai restaurants in Britain, and the distinctive Thai flavour combinations of coconut, lemongrass and galangal (similar to, but not the same as, ginger) are added to everything from steamed mussels to sandwiches. Thai spice mix sits on the supermarket shelf next to the dried chives, and in the more sophisticated supermarkets it's possible to find what would once really have been the province of restaurants – fresh lime leaves, Thai basil, nam plah.

And within Thai and south-east Asian cooking in general there are also lots of interactions and exchanges. The key spices and cooking styles extend in a series of family relationships through Laos, Vietnam, Indonesia and Malaysia as well as Thailand. Sometimes something is left out, sometimes something is changed, sometimes it's copied exactly: fish sauce in Vietnam is not the same as fish sauce in Thailand, but it's still fish sauce.

But if fusion food is a signifier of cultural history, what is it that it signifies? Tolerance, interest in other cultures, openness to new experiences, and change. We live in a world which has much of the last, but less, at times, of the first three. Food may appear trifling next to politics, economics and the other big movers of history. But at the most functional level it's the thing which makes all of those other things possible. And anyway, not all change begins with grand gestures and speeches. Being willing to sit down and eat a meal which started its history on the other side of the world might be much more important than it seems.

Down stairs, then, they went, Joseph very red and blushing, Rebecca very modest, and holding her green eyes downwards. She was dressed in white, with bare shoulders as white as snow—the picture of youth, unprotected innocence, and humble virgin simplicity. "I must be very quiet," thought Rebecca, "and very much interested about India."

Now we have heard how Mrs. Sedley had prepared a fine curry for her son, just as he liked it, and in the course of dinner a portion of this dish was offered to Rebecca. "What is it?" said she, turning an appealing look to Mr. Joseph.

"Capital," said he. His mouth was full of it; his face quite red with the delightful exercise of gobbling. "Mother, it's as good as my own curries in India."

"Oh, I must try some, if it is an Indian dish," said Miss Rebecca. "I am sure everything must be good that comes from there."

"Give Miss Sharp some curry, my dear," said Mr. Sedley, laughing.

Rebecca had never tasted the dish before.

"Do you find it as good as everything else from India?" said Mr. Sedley.

"Oh, excellent!" said Rebecca, who was suffering tortures with the cayenne pepper.

"Try a chili with it, Miss Sharp," said Joseph, really interested.

"A chili," said Rebecca, gasping. "Oh, yes!" She thought a chili was something cool, as its name imported, and was served with some. "How fresh and green they look," she said, and put one into her mouth. It was hotter than the curry; flesh and blood could bear it no longer. She laid down her fork. "Water, for Heaven's sake, water!" she cried. Mr. Sedley burst out laughing (he was a coarse man, from the Stock Exchange, where they love all sorts of practical jokes). "They are real Indian, I assure you," said he. "Sambo, give Miss Sharp some water."

The paternal laugh was echoed by Joseph, who thought the joke capital. The ladies only smiled a little. They thought poor Rebecca suffered too much. She would have liked to choke old Sedley, but she swallowed her mortification as well as she had the abominable curry before it, and as soon as she could speak, said, with a comical, good-humoured air—

"I ought to have remembered the pepper which the Princess of Persia puts in the cream-tarts in the Arabian Nights. Do you put cayenne into your cream-tarts in India, sir?"

Old Sedley began to laugh, and thought Rebecca was a good-humoured girl. Joseph simply said—"Cream-tarts, Miss? Our cream is very bad in Bengal. We generally use goats' milk;

and, 'gad, do you know, I've got to prefer it!"

"You won't like everything from India now, Miss Sharp," said the old gentleman; but when the ladies had retired after dinner, the wily old fellow said to his son, "Have a care, Joe; that girl is setting her cap at you."

"Pooh! nonsense!" said Joe, highly flattered. "I recollect, sir, there was a girl at Dumdum, a daughter of Cutler of the Artillery, and afterwards married to Lance, the surgeon, who made a dead set at me in the year '4–at me and Mulligatawney, whom I mentioned to you before dinner–a devilish good fellow, Mulligatawney–he's a magistrate at Budgebudge, and sure to be in council in five years. Well, sir, the Artillery gave a ball, and Quintin, of the King's 14th, said to me, 'Sedley,' said he, 'I bet you thirteen to ten that Sophy Cutler hooks either you or Mulligatawney before the rains.' 'Done,' says I; and egad, sir–this claret's very good. Adamson's or Carbonell's?"...

A slight snore was the only reply: the honest stock-broker was asleep, and so the rest of Joseph's story was lost for that day.

William Makepeace Thackeray (1811-1863), *Vanity Fair*

IN A PICKLE

In Japan, the traditional accompaniment to curry and rice is tsukemono (pickle). Generally a mix of daikon radish (takuan) and aubergine (karashizuke), variations include burdock (yamagoboo no shouyuzuke) and pickled cucumber (kyuuri no nukazuke).

HOT PICS

Judge Adams was determined to find out who'd raided the local balti hut.

How to run a kitchen – 13 dishes that get the curry treatment in Mrs Beeton's *Book of Household Management* (1861)

Boiled rice for curries, etc

Curried beef

Curried cod

Curried fowl

Curried fowl or chicken

Curried mutton

Curried rabbit

Curried veal

Indian curry powder (founded on Dr Kitchener's recipe)

Indian dish of fowl

Lobster curry

Mullagatawny soup

Salmon curry

FLOCK-PAPER FAVOURITES: DOPIAZA

Deciphering the curry house menu...

Not to be confused with a double pizza, this age-old favourite was known to have been served up by the kitchens of Akbar (1555-1605) – India's third Mughal Emperor's – court. In a book called the *Ain-I-Akbari* by the courtier Abul Fazl, a recipe for the dish calls for two kilograms of onions to 10 kilograms of meat. The name dopiaza is also said to mean 'twice onions' in Bengali, and in both references lies the key ingredients for the dish.

Although so much onion could seem daunting to the palate, the process used to create the dish required that half be sliced and sautéed and the other ground into a fine paste. Alongside these contrasting textures came an aromatic blend of spices – four times the amount of fresh pepper to equal measures of cumin, coriander, cardamoms, cloves plus an extra pinch of pepper and salt. A nineteenth-century pamphlet by the Oriental Translation Community also included instructions on how to make a dopiaza for expat communities who had spent time in the East. The dish had proven its longevity and lodged itself into the UK conscious even then.

Heat factor: Hot to trot.

---

144 *Number of pages in Hilaire Walden's jam-packed* Sensational Preserves *(1995) in which red curry paste appears*

THE CULINARY ADVENTURES
OF DEAN MAHOMET

Letter XXXVIII: *After leaving Calcutta, Mahomet departs India on a Dutch ship from the harbour of Belcoor, with a new country ahead of him...*

'A speck now observed in the mariner's horizon, was to him an evident sign of the impending storm, which collected with rapid increase, and bursting with resistless impetuosity over our heads, incessantly raged for three days. The howling of the tempest, the roaring of the sea, the dismal gloom of night, the lightning's forked flash, and thunder's awful roll, conspired to make this the most terrifying scene I ever experienced.

'Fair weather providentially succeeding this violent tornado, we reached St. Helena in a week, and met with the Fox English Indiaman, which received some damage by touching on a rock at some distance from the shore ... Having laid in a supply of fresh provisions and water, and proceeded on our voyage, we arrived at Darmouth [Dartmouth] in England in September 1784.'

Dean Mahomet went on to establish The Hindostanee Coffee House, the first Indian restaurant in the UK, in 1809. Proud of making such a distinctive mark, and hoping to draw custom as much from the wealthy English as his own countrymen, he advertised it in the Times on 27 March, 1811:

'Hindostanee Coffee-House, No. 34 George-street, Portman square – Mahomed, East-Indian, informs the Nobility and Gentry, he has fitted up the above house, neatly and elegantly, for the entertainment of Indian gentlemen, where they may enjoy the Hoakha, with real Chilm tobacco, and Indian dishes, in the highest perfection, and allowed by the greatest epicures to be unequalled to any curries ever made in England with choice wines, and every accommodation, and now looks up to them for their future patronage and support, and gratefully acknowledges himself indebted for their former favours, and trusts it will merit the highest satisfaction when made known to the public.'

Dean Mahomet, *The Travels of Dean Mahomet*, 1794

QUOTE UNQUOTE

We have evidence to suggest this is a national problem... and we are urging trading standards services across the UK to work with Indian restaurants in their area to ensure the amount of colorants used is within the legal limits.
Phil Thomas, food spokesman for the Trading Standards Institute, on the use of artificial colours in British curry houses in 2004

NO CURRY

We were just sitting down to dinner, and Albert's uncle was just plunging the knife into the hot heart of the steak pudding, when there was the rumble of wheels, and the station fly stopped at the garden gate. And in the fly, sitting very upright, with his hands on his knees, was our Indian relative so much beloved. He looked very smart, with a rose in his buttonhole. How different from what he looked in other days when he helped us to pretend that our currant pudding was a wild boar we were killing with our forks. Yet, though tidier, his heart still beat kind and true. You should not judge people harshly because their clothes are tidy. He had dinner with us, and then we showed him round the place, and told him everything we thought he would like to hear, and about the Tower of Mystery, and he said –

'It makes my blood boil to think of it.'

Noel said he was sorry for that, because everyone else we had told it to had owned, when we asked them, that it froze their blood.

'Ah,' said the Uncle, 'but in India we learn how to freeze our blood and boil it at the same time.'

In those hot longitudes, perhaps, the blood is always near boiling-point, which accounts for Indian tempers, though not for the curry and pepper they eat. But I must not wander; there is no curry at all in this story. About temper I will not say.

E Nesbit, *The Woodbegoods*, 1901

BURNING QUESTIONS

What is the hottest curry available in British curry houses?
Answer on page 151.

CURRY AND CHIPS: THE CAST

In the notorious 1969 ITV sitcom, the parts were played by:

Spike Milligan..Kevin O'Grady

Eric Sykes...Arthur

Geoffrey Hughes...Dick

Sam Kydd...Smellie

Kenny Lynch..Kenny

Norman Rossington..Norman

HOW TO MAKE THE PERFECT BASMATI RICE

Cooking rice isn't always as difficult as it can sometimes appear to be, if you just follow these simple steps:

1. Weigh 450g of Basmati rice and prepare one pint (600ml) of cold water.

2. Wash the rice in several changes of cold water to remove the starch, then leave it to soak for 10-20 minutes in fresh cold water.

3. Drain the rice and add it to a non-stick saucepan containing the water and a pinch of salt.

4. Bring the water to the boil, turn down the heat and cover.

5. Leave the rice to cook for 10 minutes without lifting the lid.

6. Turn off the heat and leave the rice to continue cooking in the pan for about five minutes. Don't lift the lid.

7. Remove the lid and fluff up the contents with a fork. The rice should have absorbed all of the water.

FLOCK-PAPER FAVOURITES: KORMA

Deciphering the curry house menu...

Another allusion to the cooking style, rather than the sauce, the korma (also koorma or quarama) is slow-cooked over a long period of time. In the initial stages, garlic, ginger, onion and spices (usually cardamom, cinnamon and cloves) are added to ghee or oil, to which lamb marinated in yoghurt is then braised until the combined juices condense down into a thick, aromatic sauce – what the British often derive as a korma. Although the process of marinating meat had been used long before the fifteenth-century Persian invasion of India, it was the Mughal rulers of Lucknow in the eighteenth century who can be credited with one of the UK curry house's creamy favourites.

Drawing on ingredients from the lush agricultural and dairy-rich region of the Oudh region, the Lucknavis introduced ground almonds to thicken the sauce (a classic Persian trick) plus large dollops of cream to render a cool, comforting taste and texture. Although turmeric and chillis can be added to bring depth to the sauce, the usually mild countenance of a korma has become the ideal introductory dish for curry virgins (the first British colonials certainly welcomed the addition of a gentle dish to the 'native' menu) – or those sadomasochists whose tastebuds need secret relief from one too many a vindaloo.

Heat factor: Mild and mellow.

I DO (IN TURMERIC)!

In India, it's not simply the bride-to-be that gets a pre-wedding beauty treatment – the groom also gets a makeover! And what a makeover... After he's suited and booted, the groom's family and close friends rub turmeric paste on his face. A dye, as well as an aromatic flavouring, the turmeric leaves the skin with a golden glow and is supposed to bring good luck for the newly-weds.

QUOTE UNQUOTE

In the United States, the popularity of Indian food has been slow to evolve. Somehow the rich variety of the food has been reduced to a single term: curry. Indian food is not curry powder, which originated as an English concoction, and it is not soupy, yellow mixtures.
Kathleen O'Rourke, US cookery writer

CURRY UP!

The last days of pregnancy can be a tense time, with many mothers-to-be waiting impatiently for baby to come. The enema used to be the accepted Western catalyst, although experts now render this forced flow of fluid up the nether regions a cruel and unnecessary tact. Instead, some mothers are turning to ancient Ayurvedic texts and using curry – or specifically the turmeric and hot spices in it – to speed things up. Turmeric or kanchani (meaning golden goddess) has been used for centuries in the birthing process by Indian women, and is still used today in the absence of now conventional medical help. Its effects on the liver are thought to balance the hormones out, while its properties as an analgesic helps decrease the pain of birth – working as something of a herbal epidural. Pregnant women are advised to take two or three grams of turmeric in warm milk in the run up to the big day, although because it also acts as a uterine stimulant, medical advice should be sought first. Taking turmeric during pregnancy is also said to ensure the child-to-be will have beautiful skin – another Indian name for the yellow rhizome (thickened root-like stem) is gauri or 'the one whose face is light and shining'. Back in the West, some experts believe 'curry birthing' is a myth born out of hot spices inducing the same sort of diarrhoea that often comes naturally with labour. In this vein of thinking, unless you're desperate to drop, it seems best to avoid!

Ate curries in the furthest corners of England, Wales, France, Spain and Greece

Booked a spontaneous flight to India under the premise of tracking the most authentic curry down

Ate kedgeree in bed, did tandoori for lunch and cooked a midnight feast of biryani for 12

Conducted an experiment to find the difference between Patak's, Bolst's and a home-made version of Ranald Martin's curry powder. Conclusion so far: they are all hot

Conducted another experiment to find curry's perfect drinking companion. Results as yet inconclusive, although gin and tonic is definitely up there

Became Hackney's premier curry gardener with the very first cultivation of Thai basil on Stevens Avenue (let our neighbours come forth and show us theirs)

Attempted to make the perfect rice. Finally succeeded 1,000,000 grains of rice later

Discussed the merits of curry with chefs, mechanics, musicians, cowboys, doctors, nurses, teachers, soldiers, samba dancers, politicians, artists, curators, lords, ladies and lairds

Swapped favourite recipes and practised the Indian national anthem with a keeper of books at the British Library who was on his way to curry favour with Britain's High Commissioner to India

Randomly accepted some Saffron Kitchen Goan apple chutney from a curry fan on the Paddington to Kings Cross train, who had coincidentally just been to meet its maker

Please note that although every effort has been made to ensure the accuracy of this book, the above facts may be the result of over-spiced imaginations and over-heated minds.

Spice is life... have fun with it.
Emeril Lagasse, US celebrity chef

ANSWERS

The answers. As if you needed them.

P14.   Luak: parboiled; Gaeng: boiled; Tot: fried with garlic and black pepper.

P19.   Cheese and peas.

P30.   India Pale Ale. It is brewed in London and shipped to India.

P35.   Sap: minced; Sook: raw; Yat sai: stuffed.

P47.   Dip: stir fried; Haeng: dru; Pat: stir-fried.

P53.   Ghee is a type of clarified butter from which all milk solids have been removed, meaning it can be heated to higher temperatures without risk of burning.

P64.   Tandoor. The oven is made of clay and food is grilled on charcoal at its base.

P67.   Dopiaza/Dopyaza. A second portion of raw onions is added just before serving.

P81.   Salted, sun-fried fish.

P88.   Turmeric.

P91.   Neung: steamed; Op: baked; Han: sliced.

P98.   Lassie.

P106.   Japan. Curry bread (*kare pan*) is so popular in the country that there is even a superhero named after it: 'Curry bread man'. He has a head made out of curry bread.

P118.   All three are types of Indian flat bread and used as an accompaniment to curried dishes.

P125.   A 'thali' has two different meanings in India. It refers to an Indian meal popular in the southern half of the country, which consists of a selection of different dishes, and to the wedding chain in traditional Hindu wedding ceremonies.

P133.   Vindaloo is supposed to have derived its name from its two main ingredients: vinho (wine/vinegard) and alhos (garlic).

P138.   Naam dwy, a juice made of sugar cane.

P146.   The phal. It is a hotter variation of the vindaloo, invented in Britain.

BIBLIOGRAPHY

A Journal from the year 1811 Till the year 1815, Including A Voyage To And Residence In India, With A Tour To The North-Western Parts Of The British Possessions In That Country, Under The Bengal Government. In Two Volumes, Maria, Lady Nugent

Art of South Indian Cooking, Alamelu Vairavan and Patricia Marquardt

Caribbean Cooking: A selection of West-Indian Recipes, P. De Brissiere

'Curry & Rice', On Forty Plates; Or, The Ingredients Of Social Life At 'Our Station' In India, George Francklin Atkinson, Captain, Bengal Engineers

Curry: A Tale of Cooks and Conquerors, Lizzie Collingham

Curry Culture: A very British love affair, Peter and Colleen Grove

Curry Recipes: Selected from the Unpublished Collection of Sir Ranald Martin, Mrs Jessop Hulton

Curries from the sultan's kitchen: Recipes from India, Pakistan, Burma and Ceylon, Doris Ady

Eating in Africa, Rosanne Guggisberg

Far Eastern Cookery, Robin Howe

Flavours of India, Madhur Jaffrey

Hand-Book Of India: A Guide To The Stranger And The Traveller And A Companion To The Resident, JH Stocqueler

How to grow the Tomato and 115 Ways to Prepare it for the Table, George W Carver

Indian Military Manual of Cooking and Dietary, Government of India Press

Quick After Work Curries (Curry Club), Pat Chapman

Madhur Jaffrey's Ultimate Curry Bible, Madhur Jaffrey

Sensational Preserves: 250 recipes for making and using preserves, Hilaire Walden

Spices, Salt and Aromatics in the English Kitchen, Elizabeth David

Star of India: The Spicy Adventures of Curry, Jo Monroe

Stylish Indian in Minutes: Over 140 inspirational recipes,
Monisha Bharadwaj

Thai Food, David Thomson

The All New Fannie Farmer Boston Cooking School Cookbook

The Art of Indian Cooking, Monica Dutt

The Best of British Cooking, Marika Hanbury Tenison

The Curry Secret: Indian restaurant cookery at home,
Kris Dhillon

*The Englishwoman In India: Containing Information For The
Use of Ladies Proceeding To, Or Residing In, The East Indes,
Or The Subjects Of Their Outfit, Furniture, Housekeeping, The
Rearing of Children, Duties and Wages of Servants,
Management Of The Stables, And Arrangements for Travelling.
To Which Are Added Receipts for Indian Cookery*,
By a Lady Resident

*The Essence of Japanese Cuisine: An Essay on Food and
Culture*, Michael Ashkenazi and Jeanne Jacob

*The Indian Cookery Book: A Practical Handbook to The
Kitchen in India, Adapted to the Three Presidencies; containing
Original and Approved Recipes in Every Department of Indian
Cookery; Recipes for Summer Beverages and Home-Made
Liquers; Medicinal & Other Recipes; Together with a Variety of
Things Worth Knowing*, By a Thirty-five Years Resident

The Modern Indian Restaurant Cookbook(Curry Club),
Pat Chapman

The New Curry Bible, Pat Chapman

The Raj at Table, David Burton

*What to tell the cook; or The Native Cook's Assistant, Being A
Choice Collection Of Recipes For Indian Cookery, Pastry, &c,
&c*, in English and Tamil

Book of Household Management, Mrs Beeton

The Travels of Dean Mahomet, Dean Mahomet

ACKNOWLEDGEMENTS

We gratefully acknowledge permission to reprint extracts of copyright material in this book from the following authors, publishers and executors:

Curry: The story of the Nation's Favourite Dish, Shrabani Basu
Reprinted by permission of Shrabani Basu, Sutton Publishing and HarperCollins India.

Home Life In India, John Finnemore
Reprinted by permission of Sara Doctors at the A&C Black permissions department. Thanks to Sara for researching Finnemore's copyright status.

Floyd's India, Keith Floyd
Reprinted by permission of HarperCollins Publishers Ltd. © Keith Floyd 2001.

INDEX

Widely acknowledged as *the* rice experts, Tilda is the number one selling dry rice brand in the UK, and for good reason: the company is renowned for producing only the best quality products.

Tilda Pure Basmati is the 'Prince of Rice', prized for its distinctive fragrance and delicate fluffy texture. The word 'Basmati' literally translates as 'the fragrant one' in Hindi. Basmati is unique because it grows only in the foothills of the Himalayas where it is watered by snow-fed rivers and hand-tended by dedicated farmers. The distinctive climatic conditions and soil create the exquisite delicate aroma and taste that only Pure Basmati has.

Although traditionally the authentic accompaniment to all Indian and Middle Eastern dishes, Tilda Pure Basmati rice is the ultimate long grain rice for any meal, savoury or sweet, especially casseroles and grills. It also makes superbly fragrant rice pudding.

In addition to its Original Pure Basmati rice, Tilda's dry rice range includes Brown Basmati, White and Brown Basmati, Pure Basmati and Wild Rice, Easy Cook American Rice, Giant Canadian Wild Rice, Thai Jasmine Rice, as well as Easy Cook Pure Basmati.

Tilda has also pioneered rice recipe innovation in microwave rice with the Tilda Rizazz range. The Rizazz range of two-minute microwavable rice includes an ever-growing variety of delicious rice recipes. Like all Tilda products, Tilda Rizazz is made from only the finest, quality ingredients, and being microwavable in the pack, provides a quick, simple solution for a great-tasting, healthy meal in minutes. Not only is Tilda Rizazz 100% foolproof, but you can ditch the dirty pans, which will leave you more time on your hands to do whatever your heart desires!